PRAISE FOR *THE PHYSICS OF BRAND*

"This should be your handbook for modern branding. The Physics of Brand *is what most marketing books aren't—fun to read right from the first page, engaging and generous in its trove of brand knowledge, and up-to-this-minute current with how the marketplace works today."*

—Mark Addicks

Former CMO, General Mills; Professor, Opus College of Business, University of St. Thomas

*"*The Physics of Brand *is brilliant. It's about the five senses, memories, and our experience of offerings. It's about time, space, and moments that matter. And most fundamentally, it's about branding, and within its pages you will find profound insights into your own brand."*

—B. Joseph Pine II

Bestselling Coauthor, *The Experience Economy*

"Blending a rigorous, near-scientific approach together with a sophisticated, humanistic focus on people's minds, souls, and behaviors, this book offers a comprehensive compendium of all the variables to consider for building valuable, memorable, and sustainable brands."

—Mauro Porcini

SVP & Chief Design Officer, PepsiCo

"Beautifully written, incredibly designed. This is a book that makes you look at the topic of branding with fresh eyes."

—Mark Ritson

Professor, Melbourne Business School, Australia; Columnist, *Marketing Week*

*"*The Physics of Brand *gives equal time to the risks and opportunities of developing new brands—and the massive forces at play when managing and pivoting an existing brand platform. Big kudos to this team in their thoughtful, highly creative effort to bring humanity to the data and science of brand."*

—Christopher Gavigan

Founder + Chief Product Officer, The Honest Company

"Making moments, accelerating velocity, building trust and creating value . . . The Physics of Brand *mashes classic marketing and modern reality with thought experiments to provoke experienced and aspiring marketers alike."*

—Jeff Jones

Executive Vice President & Chief Marketing Officer, Target Corporation

"Finally, a branding tome for the Donald Trump haters of the world: Truthful and lushly illustrated with a thread of wry humor. Best read at lunchtime when you are most awake and ready to intake sensible business nourishment."

—Paco Underhill

Author, *Why We Buy: The Science of Shopping*; CEO, Envirosell

THE PHYSICS OF BRAND

UNDERSTAND THE FORCES BEHIND
BRANDS THAT MATTER

AARON KELLER + RENÉE MARINO + DAN WALLACE

DESIGNED BY CAPSULE

Time is our most valuable resource. Thank you for giving some of yours.

Aaron.

Published by
HOW Books, an imprint of F+W Media, Inc.
10151 Carver Road, Suite 200, Blue Ash, OH 45242. U.S.A.
www.howdesign.com
ISBN 10: 1-4403-4267-9
ISBN 13: 978-1-4403-4267-7
eISBN 10: 1-4403-4269-5
eISBN 13: 978-1-4403-4269-1
Printed in China.
10 9 8 7 6 5 4 3 2 1

This publication is designed to provide accurate and authoritative
information with regard to the subject matter covered. It is sold with
the understanding that the publisher is not engaged in rendering
legal, accounting, or other professional advice. If legal advice or
other expert assistance is required, the services of a competent
professional person should be sought.

Many of the designations used by manufacturers and sellers to
distinguish their products are claimed as trademarks. Where those
designations appear in this book and F+W Media, Inc. was aware of
a trademark claim, the designations have been printed with initial
capital letters.

—From a *Declaration of Principles* jointly adopted by a Committee of
the American Bar Association and a Committee of Publishers and
Associations

Cover and interior design by CAPSULE.
Cover and interior illustrations by Emma Rotilie.
This book is available at quantity discounts for bulk purchases.
For information, please call 1-800-289-0963.

CONTENTS

YOU COMPLETE US

ACKNOWLEDGMENTS

The authoring and designing of a book is a work of true love. Nothing can be more motivating and much is needed to accomplish this monumental task. This clarified, more than three authors have been involved in the birth of this book. Thank you to our editor at HOW, Eileen Mullan, and our acquiring editor, Brendan O'Neill. This book would have never been completed without the support of Amelia Yingst and Nathan Henry of Cupitor, and the Capsule team: Courtney Johnson, Barry Hastings, Brian Adducci, Kitty Hart, Dan Baggenstoss, Matt Ludvigson, Emma Rotilie, and Greg Brose. This book is dedicated to Steve Marino for his courage and support.

We are also appreciative of the many friends and colleagues who helped us refine our thinking, including Jeff Brown, Steve Wallace, Stephen Baird, Nic Askew, Bruce Tait, and Pat Hanlon. Thought leaders who have influenced our work include William McDonough, Renée Mauborgne, Jon Elster, Jennifer Aakers, Marti Barletta, Alain de Botton, Pierre Lévy, E.O. Wilson, Clay Shirky, Robert Cialdini, Jean-Pierre Dubé, and Ray Kurzweil. We are particularly thankful to our colleagues Lou Carbone and Joe Pine, fellow Minnesotans who were early thought leaders in the field of customer experience.

Special thanks to our patient friends and families, and to the authors of marketing books and blogs we have read over the years. It takes a library and a social network to write a book.

Finally, thank you for reading this book. We would love to hear your feedback on Amazon or through our Twitter feeds:

Aaron Keller (@KellerOfCapsule), Dan Wallace (@Ideafood), Renée Marino (@renee_cupitor)

IT BEGAN OVER TWO PINTS

THE PREFACE

This story started fermenting in the summer of 2002, shortly after the first stock market bubble pop of the aughts. Aaron Keller and Dan Wallace sat outside the News Room at Nicollet Mall in Minneapolis, drinking beer and marveling at the pace of change in marketing, branding, and design. Advertising was in a severe depression, design was getting a seat in the boardroom, and customer experience was the new hot-button topic. Dot-com and tech stocks had crashed, closing act one of the Internet drama. We speculated on how the Internet would transform media, marketing, and branding. The whole branding system seemed like a Rube Goldberg machine, but we could only see some of the parts.

We laughed at the odd realities of our profession. There were more than 2 million registered trademarks worth trillions of dollars on global stock exchanges, supported by more than $600 billion in annual spending on research, design, promotion, and advertising. Yet, there was no consensus on why brands add value, what a brand is, or how branding even works. It seemed oxymoronic.

Then a simple insight emerged: People and brands move through time and space, and their micro-interactions are an important area left unstudied. The idea seemed elegantly simple, almost too simple, yet also deep and complex. We frankly didn't know what to do with the insight, so it sat on a shelf of our collective consciousness for a few years, occasionally pulled down and dusted off over craft beer.

Then Aaron met Renée Marino, a business appraiser who had once worked on system simulations with rocket scientists and was, at the time, intrigued by new marketing research on dynamic systems. Aaron shared the time-and-space insight with Renée, and she immediately saw how these ideas could fit together. Soon the Great Recession of 2008 gave all three of us time and space to expand the initial insight. Our fruitful explorations, research, and intense discussions turned into the book you are holding today.

Once this book is out in the world, know that we will have celebrated over three pints at the News Room. Maybe lightning will strike twice.

THE INTRODUCTION

Theoretically, brands last forever, so long as they meet up regularly with people in time and space. This book examines the times and spaces where brands and people meet. We'll look at how brands evolve in time and space, what goes on inside human brains, how social networks influence us, and why brands are valuable to the human race. Then, we'll narrow our focus and illustrate how this can produce insights into the many ways brands are valuable to brand owners and to you. Not only will you gain a new framework and a general systems perspective to help build brands, you'll also learn new ways to evaluate brands and achieve optimal branding efforts.

Most brand books focus on what brands should say or how "consumers" think and feel. This is likely the result of advertising's historical dominance in branding and the influence of market research in academics. Today advertisers are spending more money to reach fewer people, less often, for shorter amounts of time. Online advertising spending—$52 billion—exceeded cable and is nipping at broadcast television. Brands are screaming at an audience that is frequently distracted as they tap into a galaxy of information from the smartphone in their pockets and purses. And amid all this noise, people make decisions based on all of their experiences with a brand.

Big ideas aside, people are central to our thinking. We don't call people "consumers" or see customers as a target market. These terms are dusty relics of an industrial economy. Brands live or die in memory, and brands cannot live without people. So it makes sense to study how real-life human interactions with brands lead to the creation of these memories.

Customer experience and customer design are the dominant concepts in marketing today, and our insights relate directly to designed experiences—specifically moments—for people. We will also explore how the individual is influenced by the power of community. You will learn how brand owners and their handlers work to navigate this community. We'll explore three important dimensions of time that individuals experience with a brand: (1) First Moment in time; (2) Mass of Time spent with a brand; (3) Velocity of Time spent with a brand. Brands must also navigate four dimensions of space: (1) Brand Owner; (2) Brand Handlers; (3) Community; (4) Person.

You will learn how brands travel up Jacob's ladder and send out signals that people can sense. These signals are then turned into memorable moments and rolled up into memories that produce brand energy. Customers will then use this information to assess the expected utility value competing brands can provide. This is how they make purchase decisions, which leads to sales, profits, and brand value, an economic asset created by the winning brand.

Yes, you will be entering some deep waters, but don't worry. It's not as difficult as you may think.

To start out, here's an example of how this view of branding worked to build the brand SmartWool, spun from superfine merino wool. SmartWool enjoyed exponential growth over two decades with minimal advertising. SmartWool focused on creating the right signals for an engaging moment. Wool socks likely conjure up thoughts of scratchy discomfort, but once people put on a pair of these premium wool socks, their toes did not want to let go. This is the SmartWool moment. How often can you give your feet a luxurious experience for a mere $20? Cold days no longer led to frosty feet and the same socks lasted for years. Fanatical loyalists bought more pairs, spread the word, gave the socks as gifts, and talked about their happy feet with friends. Experiences, sales, and profits accumulated across time and space, resulting in a valuable and coveted brand.

Systems thinking informs our perspective. For example, systems thinking says you can gain important insights into a mechanical Swiss watch by understanding how winding the watch allows you to measure time and why you might lose a second or two each month due to gravity, magnetism, and mechanical stress. Since you can't see the inner workings of a Swiss watch, you might be convinced that if you were to add more energy with additional turns of the watch stem, you could speed up time. Likewise, without an understanding of the mechanisms that generate brand value, you might be convinced that more branding investment will always directly lead to more sales and profits. We believe systems thinking is a valuable lens for looking at the world of brands.

This book is not a guide on how to build a strong brand and dominate your market. Nor will we get deep into the black-box arts of message positioning or brand expression. Our intent is to provide you with new ways to think about brands and branding. We see a brand as a noun, an intangible asset for the owner and a container of trust for the customer. We believe branding happens whenever people and brands meet in time and space. Branding is active, a verb, the interaction between a brand and human beings. You will also gain useful mental models and consider illuminating thought experiments. For example, we'll explore a world without brands. (Hint: not a good place.) Toward the end of this book, you'll learn about the economic and social value brands provide for society along with challenges in the potholes ahead.

Our toolkit will employ mathematics and principles of physics, which have been used in the study of economics and finance for decades. Marketing is fashionably late to the party, but wearing just the right shoes. Yet according to

Professor Mark Bergen at the Carlson School of Management, "Marketing at its richest is applied economics and applied social sciences." *The Physics of Brand* will bring you to this academic party looking good and sounding smart.

As this project moved along, we came to realize that we are entering the metaphysical netherworlds of brands and branding. The following pages gaze into the human condition, how technology is transforming human culture, and the interweaving value of brands in our lives. People use brands to survive and thrive, posture and position, fulfill wants and needs, spend time and money, and save time and money. Brands have transformed our physical space and social spheres. We live in a globally connected, brave new, brand-new world.

Thank you for diving down this rabbit hole with us. Feel free to reach out when you surface. Send inquiries to info@physicsofbrand.com.

01

PHYSICS + BRANDS

THROW SEXY SUPERMODELS, SYSTEMS THINKERS,
METHODS, PROMISES, WOMEN, MEN, BIRTH, DEATH, A
MOMENT, BRAND DEFINITIONS, AND NEUROSCIENCE INTO A
LARGE CAULDRON. STAND OVER IT AND CHANT METAPHORICAL
AND PHILOSOPHICAL INCANTATIONS UNTIL A SMILE BEGINS
TO APPEAR IN YOUR MIND. YOU ARE ENTERING THE WORLD
OF PHYSICS, BRANDS, CORPORATIONS, AND PEOPLE WITH
A NEW SET OF BIFOCAL BINOCULAR LENSES. IN THE NEXT
CHAPTERS, YOUR BRAIN WILL GO PLACES YOUR BODY WILL
NEVER VISIT, AND THE NEXT TIME YOUR BODY AND BRAIN
MEET, THE NEW PERSPECTIVES YOU SHARE WILL LIKELY
BE MET WITH CURIOSITY AND RESPECT. ENJOY THE TRIP
AND LET YOUR IMAGINATION BE YOUR GUIDE.

WHAT MATTERS IN TIME

BRANDS + PEOPLE + TIME + SPACE

In ancient Greek, *physics* translates to "knowledge of nature." Physics is a natural science involving the study of matter and motion through space and time. Physics is the lens we are using to look more closely at brands. Our focus here is more on what brands do than what they say. We're applying a scientific mindset to brands and branding.

Combining the words *physics* and *brand* does create tension. Physics evokes the image of something "hard" and brand evokes the image of something "soft." Physics is science; brand is art. This will be hashed out in later chapters. Physics is logic and mathematics; brand is philosophy. Some may say that connecting physics and brand is hubris.

We will use concepts of physics to describe how brands and people move through time and space. Brands will be examined through a systems perspective, examining multiple interdependencies. Brands and people are colliding daily in time and space, and we have new tools to measure these collisions. If you can measure something, you can manage it.

That's why we've developed a new systems approach to brand that looks at how brands and people actually interact in time and space.

In the following pages, you'll gain insight into how branding activities work and why brands have value. Toward this end, we've developed three models to help you understand these interactions.

THREE SEXY SUPERMODELS

TIME, SPACE, AND JACOB

Our models are unlike the average models; they are only considered sexy through certain eyes. If you're tempted to tear out these Rube Goldberg-esque models and hang them over your desk, feel free . . . we understand.

Our Time Dimensions model (Figure 1.1) has three dimensions: (1) First Moment an individual has with a brand; (2) Mass of Time with a brand; and (3) Velocity of Time. These dimensions can apply to either the perspective of each individual or the perspective of everyone who interacts with a brand. We define the first moment not as just the initial contact or the moment a signal is received, but as the first moment a memory of the brand is created. Mass of time is an aggregation of all the time a person has interacting with the brand. And velocity is the rate of increase in time spent with a brand.

Our Space Dimensions model (Figure 1.2) has four dimensions: (1) Brand Owner, or entrepreneur or marketer, who offers culture, history, and all that resides under the umbrella of the organization; (2) Brand Handler or other entities, media, celebrities, retailers, distributors, agencies, consultants, and partners that handle the brand owner's message, product, or experience; (3) Community or the people closest to us—our family, friends, colleagues, and people we trust; (4) Person or our personal experiences buying, trying, and, perhaps, enjoying the brand.

Our Jacob's Ladder model (Figure 1.3) is where the first two models become active and take on movement. Signals within both space and time dimensions travel up what we call Jacob's Ladder, or Signals > Senses > Moments > Memories > Energy > Sales > Profits > Value. People obtain

FIGURE 1.1: TIME DIMENSIONS MODEL

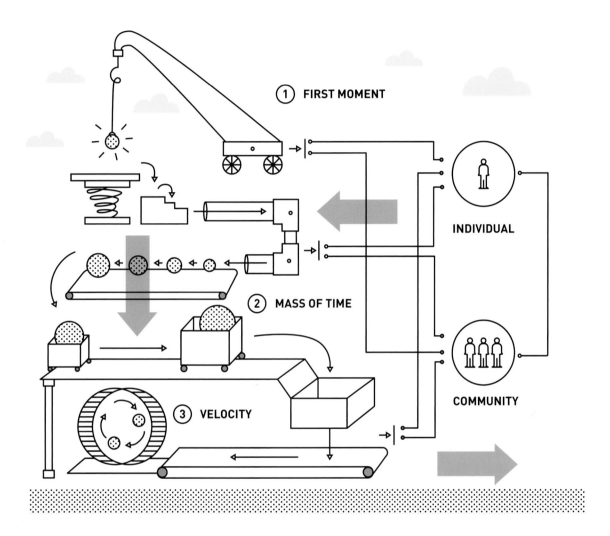

(1) THE INDIVIDUAL (YOU) HAS A FIRST MOMENT WITH A BRAND AND A MEMORY IS MADE (MARSHMALLOWS IN THIS CASE, BUT IT COULD BE WIDGETS). YOU, THE BRAND OWNER, AND BRAND HANDLERS PUT OUT SIGNALS TO OTHER MEMBERS OF YOUR COMMUNITY. (2) YOUR COMMUNITY (E.G., FRIENDS AND FAMILY) HAS ITS OWN FIRST MOMENTS AND SUBSEQUENT MOMENTS, THUS MASS OF TIME ROLLS ON AND THE MEMORY OF MARSHMALLOWS GROWS. (3) THIS ALL STARTS TO LIGHT UP YOU AND YOUR COMMUNITY BECAUSE THE TIMING OF INTERACTIONS HAS HIT A WONDERFUL ACCELERATION CURVE. MORE MARSHMALLOW MEMORIES ARE CREATED. SOMEONE BREW UP SOME HOT CHOCOLATE. HAPPY TIMES.

FIGURE 1.2: SPACE DIMENSIONS MODEL

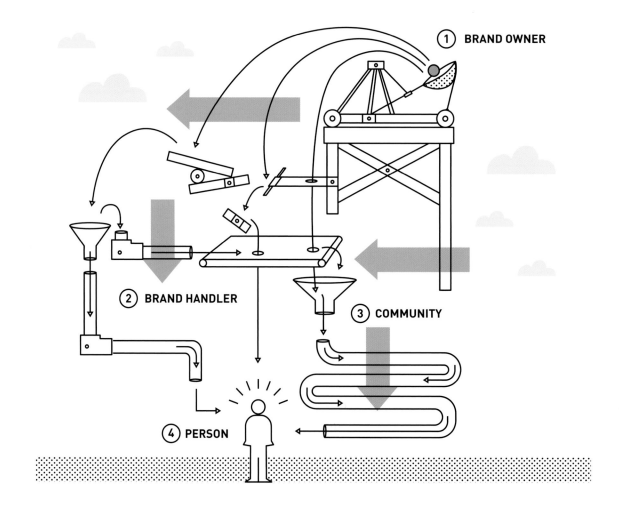

(1) HEY BRAND OWNER, LOBBING MARSHMALLOW SIGNALS OUT INTO THE PHYSICAL AND DIGITAL WORLD. WE KNOW IT'S HARD TO REACH RUBE GOLDBERG'S WIFE NINA BECAUSE SHE'S FILTERING YOU THROUGH HER COMMUNITY AND HER SKEPTICISM OF BRANDS. (2) YOUR BRAND HANDLERS SEND SIGNALS AS WELL, THOUGH MRS. GOLDBERG DOESN'T TRUST THEM MUCH. (3) WHEN HER COMMUNITY OF FRIENDS AND FAMILY RAVE ABOUT YOU, SHE LISTENS. BUT EVERYONE HAS ISSUES OF TRUST AND DISINTEREST TO RECONCILE. (4) THE FEW MARSHMALLOWS THAT MAKE THEIR WAY TO MRS. GOLDBERG HAVE A CHANCE OF FORMING A BEAUTIFUL, LASTING RELATIONSHIP OF HER REPEAT PURCHASES. IF YOU THINK THE CHALLENGES ARE EXTREME AS A BRAND OWNER, TRY SHOPPING FOR MARSHMALLOWS.

FIGURE 1.3: JACOB'S LADDER

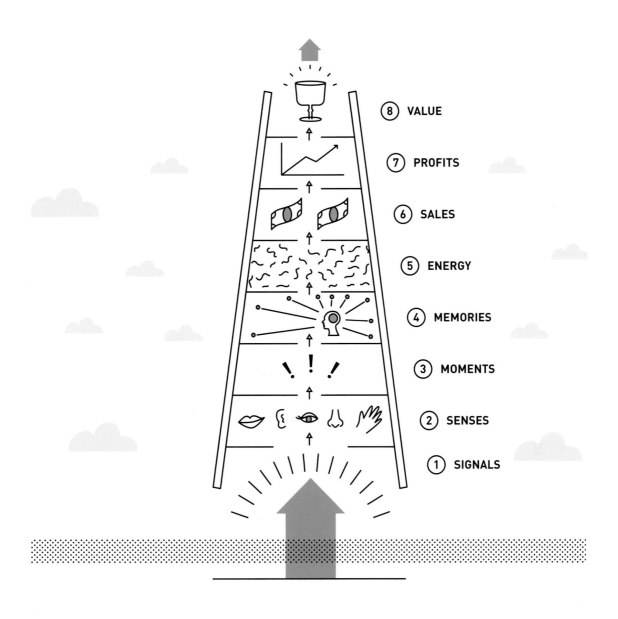

(8) VALUE

(7) PROFITS

(6) SALES

(5) ENERGY

(4) MEMORIES

(3) MOMENTS

(2) SENSES

(1) SIGNALS

THIS IS A CLIMB FOR ANY BRAND. IT STARTS WITH SIGNALS SENT IN WAVES TO OUR SENSES AND, IF THE STARS ALIGN, A MEMORABLE MOMENT IS ACHIEVED. THESE MOMENTS GATHER ENERGY THROUGH AN INCREASE IN VELOCITY LEADING TO SALES. IF THE BUSINESS MODEL IS DESIGNED RIGHT, SALES LEAD TO PROFITS AND THE CUP VALUE RUNNETH OVER. THIS VALUE IS WHAT IS CAPTURED BY BRAND OWNERS, BUT HANDLERS, COMMUNITY, AND, OF COURSE, THE INDIVIDUAL PICK UP AND KEEP THEIR OWN VALUE ALONG THE WAY. THE CUP OF VALUE TO THE OWNER IS (ALMOST) NEVER THE FULL POTENTIAL VALUE, BUT SHARING A BIT ALONG THE WAY KEEPS EVERYONE ENGAGED IN THE PROCESS OF FILLING THE BRAND OWNER'S CUP.

signals through their senses. These signals eventually reach their brains, filtered by trust apertures related to the source of the signals and social relationships. From this complex system of interactions, people create memories and accumulate energy toward a brand.

People and brand owners meet up in a dance of decisions: People bring their energy, beliefs, and desires when they consider brand offerings, and brand owners make their branding investment and pricing decisions. This dance of electricity leads to action, and action leads to sales, profits, and, eventually, value for the owner and value for the person. The Jacob's Ladder model visually describes how signals turn into moments, memories, and then brand value.

When these models are put together, you get a systems model of brand diffusion that can be used to explore thought experiments and generate ideas to improve branding and understand brand value. At this point you'll have to take these elements at their face value. We'll be swimming into the deep waters of time dimensions in Chapter 2, space in Chapters 3 and 4, Jacob's ladder in Chapters 5, 6, and 7, and the whole system in Chapter 8.

We are physical creatures as well as temporal beings. We envision sensory inputs being cross-factored with time to provide more depth to these spaces and time dimensions. Our Jacob's Ladder model is a simplification of this complex transfer. It offers similarities to the real Jacob's ladder, as the path of least resistance is the path most likely chosen. The most stable constant is time.

THE MICRO AND MACRO OF AN AURORA

AN AURORA CAN BE ENJOYED MUCH LIKE THE NORTHERN LIGHTS, BUT TO UNDERSTAND WHERE THIS OBSERVABLE LIGHT ORIGINATES YOU MUST STUDY ITS MICRO-INTERACTIONS. IT STARTS WITH A SOLAR WIND FROM THE BIG YELLOW BALL IN THE SKY. THIS ENERGY RELEASED FROM THE SUN IS A STREAM OF CHARGED PARTICLES. AS THESE PARTICLES REACH THE EARTH AND BEGIN TO INTERACT WITH THE EARTH'S MAGNETOSPHERE IT RESULTS IN AN ENERGIZING IONIZATION OF ATMOSPHERIC PARTICLES. THE EXCITATION RESULTS IN LIGHT. THE WHOLE PROCESS IS NOT WELL UNDERSTOOD AND IS STILL AN AREA OF ACTIVE STUDY. AN AURORA IS AN APT METAPHOR TO REPRESENT THE MATHEMATICS WE ARE USING TO MODEL HOW PEOPLE AND BRANDS INTERACT IN SPACE AND TIME.

THE SPECIAL GENERALISTS

OUR PROMISE

Just as the physical world and the study of physics spans subatomic particles to planets and galaxies, brands inhabit spaces in human neurons and global manufacturing, communication, and distribution systems. Similarly, just as physicists study the movement of objects in time and space, marketing leaders want to know how brands and people move through time and space.

Brands don't move in a straight line. Brands, like people, have good and bad luck as they move through time and space. Brands are capable of exponentially fast growth and equally expedited meltdowns. Humans and brands are not well suited for fixed mathematical solutions. So we use a dynamic simulation that feeds results from the current period into the next period as it crawls through time. (Hang with us here, the math will become beautiful and revealing in Chapter 8.) As you will see, brand building is an elegant balance of art and science. While you would infer a book on the physics of brand would focus on the science, we like to spend plenty of time on our art.

Physicists and marketers use similar approaches to understand reality. For example, one of the most popular brand inquiry methods is ethnographic research, face-to-face study and interaction with customers in their native environments. Like physicists, ethnographic researchers observe behaviors directly and decipher patterns. Physicists seek patterns in nature and use experiments and mathematics to explain what they see. What all market researchers have lacked is durable data. This is something we'd like to change.

Toward this end, we have designed a brand simulation tool, Aurora, to help illustrate some of the concepts throughout this book and to share on our website (*www.physicsofbrand.com*). Play around on this website as we move from the particular to the general and back again. We have drawn heavily on the math of physics to create Aurora. These and similar dynamic simulation tools are in use today by academic researchers and financial analysts. Aurora will help make these ideas more tangible and are conceptual Play-Doh to give you insights into your own brand situation.

Like particles, knowledge is best imparted in waves, not from the end of a fire hose. But before we move forward, let's all agree on what we mean by a brand.

BRAND IS EVERYTHING, BRAND IS NOTHING

WHAT IS A BRAND?

Brands are complex because they are both real and figments of our imagination. Brands were invented to replace face-to-face transactions between the customer and craftsperson. Transactions evolved from "I'll give you this goat for that pig" to "Can I really trust this jug of Roman wine?"

The original brands were primarily people and their family surnames: Farmer, Butcher, Baker, Candler, Miller, Shoemaker, Carpenter, Miner, Smith, and Gold. These names were passed on for generations, along with the craft skills these names promoted. These people were neighbors, so selling shoddy goods was risky, particularly when many of them drank a lot of beer and carried weapons.

The expansion of factories and trains turned the craft system on its head. These modern inventions rapidly widened the distance between producer and customer. When the producer is in another state or country, it's harder to get your money back or exact justice if the product harms you. This modern production system needed a way to establish trust. Enter, stage right, modern branding.

People have always needed containers for trust. We are genetically wired to weigh risks two-to-one over rewards. Brands evolved to become containers of trust. Then brands vaulted forward in the late 1800s when the United Kingdom and France gave makers of goods the legal rights to own a brand name in order to protect people from fraud. Today, these intellectual property rights to brands have become containers of great value for corporations.

Historically, the economy "lit it up" as factories, railroads, and the printing press accelerated human-to-human transactional bonds. The late 1800s to mid-1900s were a time of great invention, and brands largely sold themselves. Everyone wanted the new wonders of indoor plumbing, central heating and cooling, electric light, phones, automobiles, vacuum cleaners, dishwashers, laundry soap, and all the inventions of a modern age.

In the United States after World War II, in order to prevent future economic crises and promote trade, there was a pragmatic effort by government, finance, and industry to create a society of manufacturers and consumers. Over time, puritan thrift had to compete with the ethic of conspicuous consumption. This change was made real at most fairgrounds where, after World War II, Machinery Hill was overrun by corndogs and carnival rides.

Returning World War II marketers rebranded

"customers" as "consumers," and adopted military terminology such as identifying "target" markets and market "penetration." Mass media fueled brand growth in a consumption-driven culture. This depersonalization of brands was at odds with the original purpose of brands filling the void in the lost relationship between buyer and seller. Over time, Johnson the grocer, Dayton at the local clothier, and Frank at the hardware store were replaced by big-box retailers stuffed floor to ceiling with an abundance of brand choices, loud promotions, and minimal staff.

Mass advertising accelerated "consumer" brands after World War II, and soon, as substantial product invention subsided, the ad agency Mad Men started to promote nuanced differences between brands. Producers and advertisers began to focus on small improvements and aspirational aspects of products, such as whiter teeth, fresher breath, or smoother hair. There was an overt effort to focus on human anxieties, and the volume of commercial messages increased.

Over time the noise grew, first through the introduction of cable TV, and now through the pre-Cambrian explosion of content marketing on the Internet. Older people are often confused and upset by this changing media landscape, while younger people are opting out of traditional media altogether and blocking online ads. Meanwhile, we're all just a Google search away from brutal product reviews and shopping guides.

Whether it was the booze or the height of the office towers, the Mad Men of Madison Avenue eventually degraded the trust between brands and people. They spoke down to the women, who make 80 percent of household purchases, at a time when highly educated women took to the streets demanding equal rights. These same women helped fuel the consumer and environmental protection movements running parallel to their efforts. No wonder trust in brands has suffered a slow, sad decline. Some reports, coming right out of the advertising agency Y&R, report a 50 percent drop in trust in the past decade.

Part of this drop in trust can be traced back to how advertising agencies made money in the Mad Men era. Agencies used to get a 15 percent commission (some countries call this a kickback) from the mass media for all the TV, radio, and magazine ads they bought. Ad agencies, publishers, and broadcasters worked together to convince brand owners to advertise more, even though nobody knew—or does know— exactly how mass brand advertising works. In many cases, it's difficult to know whether brand advertising works at all. Because mass-media advertising was so profitable, ad agencies called this work "above the line" and convinced clients that mass-media brand advertising was the best way to build brands. This system did not focus on customers, and inefficiency was actually rewarded, and this party never stopped.

"Below the line" expenses included market research, in-store merchandising and sampling, staff training, special events, sponsorships, press initiatives, sales promotion, point-of-sale displays, design, and direct marketing. If they were around at that time, websites, blogging, social media, and pay-per-click ads would also be considered below the line. Our models and research indicates that below-the-line activities are generally more effective than mass-media advertising. This insight is a signpost identifying the end of an era.

A new age is being born. Marketing theorists pontificate about "good, better, best" and how "consumers" only desire a choice between two meaningful options. As the ghosts of cable TV fade in memory, the fragmentation of mass media and the invention of the Internet have splintered the structure holding mass brand advertising at the top of the marketing mix. Online ratings and the wisdom of the crowd are superseding brand messages. The world is becoming more transparent and the message more difficult to control. Woe be to those brands with too many one-star reviews on Amazon, Yelp, or Glassdoor.

There are still times when traditional mass advertising can be worth the tremendous expense involved. When a brand like Apple has a dramatic high-margin innovation that requires rapid adoption nationally or globally—think iPod, iPhone, iPad, and Apple Watch—mass advertising can be used offensively. In contrast, defensive brand advertising is often used by widely distributed legacy brands serving people with old media habits. Think of Viagra, Charles Schwab, and Olive Garden. Mass-media advertising can also be used tactically for offers and events, or to make direct sales.

The concept of a brand is changing as well. The word *brand* was once reserved for national names like Ivory Soap, Coca-Cola, Miller Lite, and Life Cereal. Now, we see brands as retailers (Amazon, Etsy, and Costco), celebrities (Jimmy Fallon, Reese Witherspoon, and PewDiePie), institutions (Harvard, Wikipedia, and the United Nations), and even communities (Ireland, Reddit, and the Roquefort area of France). And, as if this wasn't enough, we now have a "personal brand" movement finding traction in a growing population of independent or freelance individuals. These individuals are projected to make up 34 percent of the United States workforce by 2020.

People have a deep need to belong and brands signal commonalities worth sharing, attracting like-minded people. Brands segment us into categories just as people use brands to sort themselves into categories. Brands are used to attract potential mates and business partners; global brands are transcending cultural barriers, becoming symbols of an interconnected world. In a world of choice, needs have become wants. People use brands for status, belonging, stimulation, and diversion. Life is filled with existential angst and great difficulties. Brands provide an escape or diversion from reality.

We have moved from friends and family interacting with the baker, the butcher, and the

MEN DO HAVE GREAT INFLUENCE OVER BUSINESS-TO-BUSINESS PURCHASES IN THE WORK ENVIRONMENT, ALTHOUGH WOMEN ARE TYPICALLY HEAVILY INVOLVED IN THESE DECISIONS AS WELL. IN GENERAL, MEN SEEM TO WANT TO HEAR WOMEN'S VOICES BEFORE MAKING IMPORTANT DECISIONS.

NOW THAT WE KNOW WHO DOES THE BUYING, LET'S EXPLORE WHY SHE BUYS, WHY HE OCCASIONALLY BUYS, AND START BY DEFINING A BRAND AND BRANDING. LADIES AND GENTS, IT'S IMPORTANT THAT WE ARE ON THE SAME PAGE WITH THESE TWO IMPORTANT WORDS.

carpenter to the retailer, brand owner, and the employee. And now, through the Internet, we see a movement pulling us back to the butcher, baker, and carpenter—a world in which we can have a trusting relationship with real people through Internet platforms. At the same time we have a societal need for brands that can use economies of scale to provide good deals to the individual and profit to the producer.

"THE CONSUMER ISN'T AN IDIOT—SHE'S YOUR WIFE"

WOMEN RULE THE QUEENDOM

Women control 80 percent of all household purchases and 95 percent of all discretionary household purchases. Then consider that 70 percent of the economy is household expenditures. Sorry guys, you are not the kings. Mad Man David Ogilvy came up with the quote we used as the above title, and it's clear Lord Ogilvy understood the dangers of calling women consumers. Apple evangelist Guy Kawasaki doesn't believe it even makes sense to ask men what they think when doing market research. Guy says men don't matter and they provide lousy insights anyway.

We thought of calling this section the "politically incorrect part of the book," and

it's a volatile topic for sure, but not a single sane marketer can ignore this topic. The raw numbers are too compelling. The reasons for the household division of labor are likely rooted in history and biological differences between men and women. If you want to get deep into the subject, read *Marketing to Women* by Martha (Marti) Barletta.

The truth is, the reality of gender is very complicated, and while we all naturally use stereotypes to draw hard lines and simplify gender, the lines are fluid. What we do know is that gender is always top of mind. Harvard linguist Steven Pinker did a study of multiple languages to find out what is important to people. Pinker discovered core human interests are our common connections, relative social status, and gender.

A BRAND-DEFINING MOMENT

BRAND, DEFINED

Brands have already removed the human-to-human interaction from commerce. The power struggle between retailer and manufacturer in the 1990s has now been turbocharged with Amazon, using "brick and mortar" as their showroom and offering instant photo scan and one-click ordering for instant gratification. Even before the Internet, retailers and channel partners had started becoming the faces of brands.

Many people have forgotten the original purpose of a *brand*. A brand is a container of trust. We may be able to blame our society's prolific and sometimes confusing interpretations of the word brand, leading to a gaggle of brand definitions. As we scoured the definitions, there were a handful we pulled to help frame the discussion. Here are some definitions of brand to consider:

• "A PERSON HAS A SOUL. A PRODUCT HAS A BRAND." —JENNIFER KINON, DESIGNER, EDUCATOR, AND COFOUNDER OF OCD (ORIGINAL CHAMPIONS OF DESIGN)

This is a simple way to get the idea of a brand and why we (as humans) have invented this concept. When done well, you can sense the soul of a brand when you experience it.

- "BRAND IS A COLLECTION OF PERCEPTIONS IN THE MIND OF THE CONSUMER."
—PAUL FELDWICK

Where they reside is not a definition really, but it is important because we will be talking about the human brain, memory, and how sensory experiences impact memory.

- "A BRAND IS ESSENTIALLY A CONTAINER FOR A CUSTOMER'S COMPLETE EXPERIENCE WITH THE PRODUCT AND COMPANY."
—SERGIO ZYMAN, AUTHOR OF *THE END OF ADVERTISING AS WE KNOW IT*

The idea of a container and the experience (used here to represent historical interactions versus specific designed experiences) makes this definition closest to how we are framing the discussion. This also points to the central nature of customer experience.

- BRANDS ARE WHAT THEY DO, NOT WHAT THEY SAY." —NICK BELL, NICK BELL DESIGN

We admire the focus on how brands behave (truth is in behaviors) versus how they communicate. But in order to know if the behavior is truthful, we need to hear what a brand communicates. If what a brand says and does is in alignment, then we have a more authentic brand.

- A BRAND IS "THE INTANGIBLE SUM OF A PRODUCT'S ATTRIBUTES: ITS NAME, PACKAGING, AND PRICE, ITS HISTORY, ITS REPUTATION, AND THE WAY IT'S ADVERTISED." —DAVID OGILVY, AUTHOR OF *OGILVY ON ADVERTISING*

There are many more definitions. We counted over twenty-five at the time of this writing.

The battle for brand supremacy happens in books such as this, so to add ours to this list we figured it better be worthy.

- OUR DEFINITION: A BRAND IS A VESSEL FOR MEANING AND TRUST, FUELED BY EXPERIENCES.

A brand is an extension of you. Just as you collect meaning, understanding, and attributes over time, so does a brand. Leaders in your life influence you dramatically, and the same goes for a brand. The people who are closest to you know you best and are often most honest with you, and the same goes for a brand. When you buy a new wardrobe and shave the appropriate body parts you feel better, and the same goes for a brand.

Brands exist to ensure trust, deliver meaning, and provide economic and social value over physical and social distance. What's been lost in much of modern branding is the human part of the equation.

THE ACT OF INFUSING HUMAN ENERGY

BRANDING NEEDS A REBRAND

The active word coming from brand is branding. The act of branding has two sides: inside and outside. Inside an organization, branding is alignment of the culture to the brand's promise. As J.W. Marriott said, "If you take care of your people, your people will take care of your customers, and your business will take care of itself." The effort to align internal culture with external brand reality has become more relevant in the age of the Internet, where brands deal with social media and inside behaviors leaking to outside media sources. When someone with 50,000 followers on Twitter becomes a media source, leaks will happen.

Transparency is more than a new buzzword. It's a new reality. What happens inside your walls will easily slip outside. Even Apple and the NSA are not immune. The strongest brands start inside

THOUGHT EXPERIMENT

HOW WOULD VIDEO CAMERAS IN THE OFFICE ENVIRONMENT CHANGE BEHAVIOR? WHAT IF YOU KNEW YOUR GRANDMA COULD BE WATCHING?

first, and then move outside. Strong brands are aligned in who they are, what they say, and what they do.

In contrast, the external activity known as branding has been tarnished and minimized. The minimizers have proclaimed branding as an effort to build the corporate or product brand with no concern for building sales, when in actuality, the efforts may have lacked the proper metrics. The advertising metrics of impressions, reach, and frequency are broken, and the fact that public relations uses a derivative of these metrics only pushes us further in the wrong direction.

*offer only eligible as long as brands exist in space and time and in the memories of individuals and communities alike.

1$ OFF!! YOUR NEXT COUPON*

The reality is tactics such as interruption, trickery, discounts, coupons, payment for loyalty, and price reductions rarely fit under the branding umbrella. A focus on branding should take attention away from price onto other attributes of the offering. These "nonbranding" activities have become highly addictive to marketers because they have two shiny features: more metrics and instant motivations to buy. The outcome of decades of price-driven efforts is a category that looks more like a slurry of commodities than brands.

Consider the case of Groupon, which sells 50-percent-off coupons in an effort to generate energy, revenue, and future loyalty. What was the observable behavioral outcome from putting out a Groupon discount with your brand? People came, shopped, engaged, and purchased, but not in an economically sustainable manner. The effort causes a surge in traffic to a brand, sometimes

causing operational headaches and certainly lost margin. Existing brand loyalists must then deal with a crowd descending upon their experience at a discounted price they did not receive. Groupon customers, loyal to the Groupon brand, enter the experience at a discounted rate, and if these bargain hunters return, the cheapskates need to reconcile paying full price for something they originally experienced on discount. The Groupon method is a prime example of how to use price to diminish brand loyalty, on a mass customized scale, while building the Groupon brand exponentially.

Internal and external marketing professionals alike have long relied on the phrase "we know branding is important because people say it is, but we struggle to measure how important." And when they are asked how to build a brand, many marketers focus first on advertising and then all the rest of the disciplines.

If you're a young marketing professional, it isn't your fault. You were likely given a dated education from your academic institution. Why? Because your academic textbook likely still uses "Integrated Marketing," and a good three-quarters of its content is "advertising" or "promotions" with a small mention of marketing efforts not involving exotic shoots, models, catered lunch, and multimillion-dollar media-buying budgets.

Take a look at the most recent edition of *Advertising and Promotion: An Integrated Marketing Communications Perspective*, where content bias toward traditional advertising (TV, print, radio) outranks levers like experience design, product design, public relations, digital, social media, point-of-purchase, and packaging, at a 3:1 ratio. They conflate advertising to be marketing in the same way Hollywood films represent entertainment media, largely ignoring television, gaming, and online media channels, which are, by time involvement and financial return measures, more popular than the movie industry. The video game industry, by itself, represents $24 billion in revenue versus $10 billion for movies.

In a world that has evolved beyond the Don Draper 1960s world of advertising, textbooks still reflect the veneer and glitz of a world that has already changed by leaps and bounds. How might these textbooks explain the branding of GoPro, Airbnb, Uber, Costco, Starbucks, and Lululemon Athletica, all built without much advertising at all? A thoughtfully designed experience that provides real value is certainly a big part of the answer.

THE WORKING END OF A BRAND

BRANDING, DEFINED

If the brand is the asset and a noun, branding is the act of putting the asset to work. Branding is a verb. Here are some definitions of branding worthy of commentary:

- "BRANDING IS THE BUSINESS OF FINDING AND CELEBRATING THE MOST INTERESTING TRUTH ABOUT A GOOD OR SERVICE IN A WAY THAT THE WORLD WON'T HATE." —DAFNA GARBER, A MINNESOTA NATIVE WHO NEVER FORGOT HER ROOTS. THIS IS AN INTERESTING AND HONEST VIEW FROM THE WORLD OF ADVERTISING ABOUT THE CHALLENGES THAT ARE FACED WHEN ADVERTISING PROFESSIONALS TRY TO MAKE THE TRUTH INTERESTING.

- "BRANDING IS THE ART OF ALIGNING WHAT YOU WANT PEOPLE TO THINK ABOUT YOUR COMPANY WITH WHAT PEOPLE ACTUALLY DO THINK ABOUT YOUR COMPANY. AND VICE-VERSA." —JAY BAER, CONVINCE & CONVERT (*WWW.CONVINCEANDCONVERT.COM*), AUTHOR WITH AMBER NASLUND OF *THE NOW REVOLUTION*. THIS DEFINITION LIMITS BRANDING TO ALIGNMENT, WHEN BRANDING CAN SUGGEST NEW USES FOR A PRODUCT OR NEW OCCASIONS OF USE, OR TRY TO APPEAL TO DIFFERENT MARKETS. ALIGNMENT IS A PASSIVE APPROACH TO BRANDING, NOT A LEADERSHIP APPROACH. HOWEVER, FOR MANY LEGACY BRANDS, THIS IS ALL THEY CAN DO.

- "'BRANDING' IS WHAT LAZY AND INEFFECTIVE MARKETING PEOPLE DO TO OCCUPY THEIR TIME AND LOOK BUSY." —DAVID MEERMAN SCOTT, BESTSELLING AUTHOR OF *REAL-TIME MARKETING AND PR*. IF WE CAN'T MAKE FUN OF OUR HUMAN NATURE, THEN THE HOCKEY STICK ON A GROWTH CHART IS PROTRUDING FROM THE WRONG PLACE.

Just as in the definitions of brand, we see wide variances in the word *branding*. The number of versions misplacing "brand" with "branding" is both astonishing and embarrassing to anyone in the marketing profession. The important pieces in these definitions center on movement or activity. While the brand is the vessel or asset as some refer to it, branding is the act of lighting the rockets or getting the propellers moving.

We offer our definition as: Branding is the act of filling a brand with meaning and promises kept.

So now we've covered the vessel and the activity, and we will be covering the energy fueling brands in the coming chapters. For that matter, the majority of this book is centered on understanding the sources of energy. We are proposing to fix the imbalance and get back to why brands were invented and how leaders and managers should treat them.

We have developed a new framework for understanding why brands have value and a new approach to building strong brands. First, we need to fix some misperceptions, contradictions, and misunderstandings in order to lay the floorboards for this new perspective to stand atop.

IT'S ALIVE! OH MY, WHAT HAVE I DONE?

A BRAND IS BORN

The curious question, "When is a brand alive?" has been batted around by our triad for a while and was even sent out into the social media universe to the "marketing crowd." Sadly, the

THOUGHT EXPERIMENT

WHY DOES YOUR BRAND ENGAGE WITH PEOPLE IN SPACE AND TIME?

report back is grim. Most people who have marketing, design, or creative in their title say a brand is only a brand when it reaches a certain size. Which leaves us with a dilemma: When is a brand a brand? When 10,000, 100,000, or 1,000,000 people have heard of it? Or is birth defined by revenue? And then how much revenue do you need to be a brand?

These empirical thresholds are without merit, as you can find small brands with 10,000-person audiences that are highly successful ventures. An example is contemporary artwork by Damien Hirst, who sells diamond-encrusted skulls and embalmed sharks for $10–90 million. If your margins are high enough, a small brand can do just fine.

For revenue, consider when Facebook agreed to buy Instagram for $1 billion even though they had no revenue. What Instagram did have was a large, fast-growing community. What you discover if you've debated the birth of a brand is this fundamental fact: Moms know best.

ASK YOUR MOM

SHE KNOWS BRANDING BEST

Yeah, that's right. You start a new venture in your garage—pardon the Silicon Valley stereotype here—and somewhere in the discussions you've come up with a name, registered a domain, and told your mom. She approved of the name and you're off to the races.

As your first (slightly biased) audience member, your mom gives your brand life when you say, "Mom, our new business is called blopityboop and our Facebook page goes live tomorrow." And she responds with a typical, "Okay sweetie, that's nice, have fun." Or maybe she asks what on earth you are thinking. Either way, when mom knows your brand exists, you have a brand.

Your government sees it a bit differently depending on the country where you're starting. In the United States you'll need to register the business with the state where you'll have annual meetings and pay taxes—though don't mistake this as a U.S. trademark. You'll also want to register with the U.S. Patent and Trademark Office. When it comes to trademark, laws differ by country, but the idea is the same. Be sure to tell the federal government that you'd like to treat this as something you own and you'd like to set some reasonable intellectual property fences. If you're not setting up an intellectual cattle ranch overlapping someone else's ranch (naming your new brand after another brand in the same category), you should be good. And for those of you who name brands, this is a gross simplification of the hardest creative task. No disrespect intended, just shortened for convenience.

The important piece is knowing your brand is alive much sooner than most think. And similar to raising a child, those early years are critical. You are a parent, and with this birth comes responsibility and opportunity.

TO KNOW LIFE, YOU MUST ALSO KNOW DEATH

IS A BRAND DEAD?

Here's where modern brand management gets creepy and interesting all at once. When does a brand actually die? For example, Enron is alive and well as a brand, but it is dead as a living corporation. Try purchasing the domain Enron .com, and it will come at a price far beyond free. For those who thought, "You have to have revenue to have a brand," but saw that isn't so, you might have guessed that it's also not the case with the death of one. If we define a brand as something living in our collective memory, then brands die slowly. In our digital future a brand may never leave our collective consciousness, therefore never die.

This, of course, doesn't stop the sideline commentators from making lists of brands that will die in the coming one, three, or five years. Don't worry if you work for a brand on the list because, if the brand has enough international awareness to appear on the list, then death is a long way off. Currently some of the brands making the list include LivingSocial, the Tribune Media Company, JCPenney, BlackBerry, Sears, Quiznos, the WNBA, Red Lobster, Sony, and Volvo.

If you authentically understand a common definition of a brand, none of these brands will expire for at least a century. When it comes to a brand, life comes early and death may never happen. Brands and corporations are theoretically immortal.

THIS IS YOUR BRAIN ON BRANDS

BRAIN SCIENCE

What do we know about the brain relative to brands and marketing? More importantly, what don't we know? These are also two important boundaries for this discussion, because when we think we know everything, branding starts to seem as simple as flipping on a light switch.

WE ARE AT A NEW FRONTIER OF RAPID DISCOVERIES ABOUT THE BRAIN, ON THE SCALE OF THE HUMAN GENOME DISCOVERIES IN THE 1990S. FMRI BRAIN SCANS AND NEW BIG-DATA TOOLS ARE ALLOWING SCIENTISTS TO UNDERSTAND WHAT PARTS OF OUR BRAINS WORK IN RESPONSE TO WHAT STIMULI.

Other times, the complexity is overwhelming and therefore impossible for an organization to learn and understand.

One of the most powerful computers in the world today, the Titan at the Oak Ridge National Laboratory, consumes 8.2 megawatts of power. That's 8.2 million watts of power filling over 4,300 square feet of physical space. The human brain occupies 1,130 cubic centimeters and uses 12 watts of power, about one-third of your refrigerator light bulb. Yes, the computers may win in the end, but today's computers are only about as smart as a mouse.

How does the brain do so much more with so little? Shortcuts. One of the ways our brain works so efficiently is through what we call heuristics, which come from thousands of years of evolution and learning. Brands rely upon heuristic shortcuts in order to be valuable. We don't need to use more of our 12 watts to process each decision if we know and trust the brand. Brands make our lives easier, until they don't.

If you're the brand of choice, you own a majority share of the patterns in the brains of the most people and your mission is to keep the patterns in your favor. If you're the up-and-coming brand, then breaking patterns or creating dissonance is your mission. You need to block off, reroute, or change the heuristics customers are using and then reroute them in your favor. Attaching a $10 bill to the end of a stick to lead the customer to another shortcut is one way, but then you're giving up margin and doing anti-branding work. Finding a retail partner who will give preference (ideal shelf space) to your brand and perhaps drop it onto the cover of its weekly circular may cost less and deliver more pattern breakage. We can see our brains light up to images of puppies and babies. Of course, we don't need an fMRI to know these images have emotional appeal. More important, we are learning about which parts of the brain control certain aspects of human behavior, memory, and sensory input. And this is where we need to resist the urge to take the leap toward predictive thoughts. Just because we can see inside our noggins doesn't mean we can predict what dad will do when walking down the grocery aisle looking for the right bottle of laundry detergent. He is still an unpredictable beast and we need to respect that fact.

As we gain a greater grasp of our own brains, we will deepen our understanding of brands. Without memory, a brand does not exist, so it is important for the owner of a brand to develop an understanding of the history of how and when memories were created and in how many brains. For example, Lance has five memorable moments of Miller Lite and Sam has ten. Lance's memories include bike riding across Iowa and involve the color of the can and the taste and the feel of the cold brew after a long day on a bike. Sam's memories are of his uncle fishing, which was not a pretty sight and is the primary reason why he now only consumes craft beer. These numbers would be a part of an archaeological dig into the formation of this brand's memories, but we also need to understand sentiment and motivations that were a part of the memories.

If we can uncover sentiment, we can better understand Sam's motivations for leaving the brand and perhaps bring him back. Brand owners are capturing data on memory, sentiment, and motivations at an exponential rate today. Combined with greater understanding of the inner workings of our brain, we may just yet put a blue can back in Sam's beer koozie.

"HUMAN BEING" INTO A "CONSUMER DOING"

TRANSFIGURING PEOPLE

As mentioned earlier, the U.S. government and industry cooperated to thwart economic recessions and compete with communism by moving from a producer society to consumer society after the Second World War. The United States started as a novice, but quickly became an expert at buying and consuming, and as a result, brands have become a religion of sorts. In the process, people have come to see themselves more as human doings than human beings. One thing is for sure: It's been great for the storage industry.

Countermovements push in new directions. Today, many activist groups are pushing to adjust our collective perspective on consumption. The environmental and minimalism movements are standing side by side with the design movement. When more time is spent on design, the solutions are likely to be more sustainable and elegant. Investing in systems design can reduce cost and waste while increasing customer utility and profits to the brand owner. Modern environmentalists like William McDonough come from the design world and offer a new model of a responsible consumer paired up nicely with responsible brands. While this is a mere garden hose feeding the ocean, the volume of awareness and interest is growing and likely to continue growing.

PEOPLE TO PEOPLE

B2B, B2C, C2C, AND P2P

The constructs of business-to-business (B2B), business-to-consumer (B2C), and person-to-person (P2P) markets play an interesting role in our thinking. We are just arriving at a time when brand owners in the B2B world are managing their brands. They've always been there, but it was just not recognized because of statements like, "We don't have a brand; we are all business to business." This brings about the question, "Does your business interact with human beings?" And the paired question, "Do you have a reputation in your industry?" You don't have to recognize a brand to have one, but you do need recognition in order to properly manage a brand.

In the business-to-consumer world, there has been a long history of seeing the importance of brand, but not seeing the customer as a human being. This deficiency is just as problematic as a business-to-business brand owner not seeing their brand sitting on the conference room table in front of them. If you only see a human being as a consumer, shopper, buyer, or other transactional title, you're missing a chance at creating depth and dimension. The advantage many business-to-business brand owners have is a face-to-face transaction in which a brand has brought the relationship together, and then human beings close the deal.

The next level of understanding is the human level. Until the computers and robots take over and all transactions take place digitally, we are still in a human-to-human world. We transact between human beings across many cultures, belief systems, and geographic regions, but in all cases, commerce is between human beings.

TO STUDY BRANDS IS TO STUDY HUMAN BEINGS

GAZING INTO YOUR NEIGHBOR'S NAVEL

We, as a human race, have created brands to improve trust in the transactions that are transported across space and time. We can't avoid brands in our life. Just try to spend a day without seeing or consuming brands in any form. It is impossible unless you are meditating in a cave in Nepal.

Brands are not going away; they are living, moving, and evolving entities. As average citizens, it is imperative we understand how brands play a role in our lives. Only after better understanding this can we change how brands are managed for good.

Look deep into the history of any brand and you discover the origin, founders, and even the moment they were given life. There are many correlations to a human life and how the early years of life are so very essential to later success. Raising kids is a challenge. It's important to embed the right values early in their history. They grow up fast, leave the house, and eventually find themselves with a moral decision to make. If you've given them the right tools to deal with whatever event they have to confront, then they will have a chance to survive and thrive.

REMEMBER THE ONE ABOUT THE BRAND PHYSICIST?

CONCLUDING MEMORIES

LIKE ANY GOOD CONTENT YOU CONSUME, THERE ARE THREADS THAT WEAVE IT ALL TOGETHER. MEMORY IS A KEY ELEMENT OF OUR THINKING, SO TO HELP YOU REMEMBER WHAT YOU'VE LEARNED, WE'LL WRAP UP WITH SOME KEY TAKEAWAYS. THE FOLLOWING WON'T REPLACE THE RICHNESS OF READING A CHAPTER, BUT WILL PROVIDE SHORTHAND TO SHARE IDEAS WITH OTHERS. THE MOST IMPORTANT TAKEAWAYS ARE THE PRACTICAL APPLICATIONS THESE IDEAS STIMULATE IN YOUR MIND. THIS IS MERELY OUR WAY TO HELP DESIGN A MEMORABLE MOMENT FOR YOU, OUR COVETED READER.

(1) Brands and people interact in time and space, and these are the most important intersections of study. Brand communication theories are good and useful, but in the real world, brands and people mix it up in time and space. It's good to be sensible and grounded in the real world.

(2) Brands operate within complex social systems, with people at the center, surrounded by trusted communities, followed by not-so-trusted handlers for brands (e.g., ad agencies, PR agencies, suppliers, media, retailers) and on the outside of the circle, brand owners. Our three dimensions of space make clear the social challenge brands face. She is the queen.

(3) Brands send out signals into the world that are sensed by people. If designed, these signals are incorporated into emotionally compelling and memorable moments. Over time moments can turn into long-term memories and habits. Many positive memories with many people lead to brand energy, sales, and profits. We call this our Jacob's ladder of brand energy.

(4) Brands are born in time, and the length and circumstances of these beginnings can help give a brand credibility. People experience time in moments, and designing experiences that lead to these moments is critical to brand success. Moments roll up into a mass of time spent with brands as they become successful and people develop buying habits. Fast-moving brands create a special kind of velocity and brand energy that energizes viral proliferation within communities. We call these different takes on our dimensions of time.

(5) We experience time through our many senses. The most known and noticed five senses have special properties that are of particular importance to certain brand categories, which if well-designed, can deliver engaging and memorable experiences.

02

TIME + BRANDS

AFTER READING THIS CHAPTER, YOU'LL LIKELY WANT
PEOPLE TO SPEND MORE TIME WITH YOUR BRAND. THINK
OF YOURSELF AS A HIKER WHO PUTS NEW IDEAS IN YOUR
BACKPACK. AND, AS WITH THE STEPS OF A HIKER, THE
MORE AWARE YOU ARE OF YOUR TEMPORAL AND PHYSICAL
SURROUNDING, THE SOONER YOU GET TO YOUR DESTINATION.
INTERACTIONS IN TIME AND SPACE TAKE ON NEW
IMPORTANCE IN THIS CHAPTER. YOU WILL STORE NEW IDEAS
IN YOUR BACKPACK THAT REVEAL THE IMPORTANCE OF AGE,
ENGAGEMENT, EXPERIENCES, AND PROPERLY DESIGNED
MOMENTS. TIME IS A CONSTANT THAT HELPS BRANDS
MOVE THROUGH SPACE.

ALBERT IS A BRAND?

THE ICONIC GERMAN-BORN PHYSICIST ALBERT EINSTEIN DIED MAKING A LARGE DENT IN THE UNIVERSE OF SCIENCE AND CULTURE, WHILE PROVING TIME AND SPACE ARE KISSING COUSINS. HE LEFT $1 MILLION TO HIS FAMILY. THIS, OF COURSE, PALED IN COMPARISON TO THE BRAND HE PASSED ON TO HIS FAMILY. THE ROYALTIES FOR BABY EINSTEIN ALONE PAY $12 MILLION PER YEAR, WHICH IS A RATHER VALUABLE BRAND BY MOST STANDARDS. ALBERT DEFINED A NEW STANDARD FOR SMART. HIS IRREVERENT PERSONALITY WAS DEPICTED AS "MAD SCIENTIST," BUT IN TRUTH, IT MADE HIS EXTREME INTELLECT MORE ACCESSIBLE. EINSTEIN IS A BRAND MANY PEOPLE ARE PROUD TO INTRODUCE TO THEIR BABIES ON THE HOPE THEY WILL PICK UP JUST A BIT OF HIS CAPACITY FOR CREATIVE AND CRITICAL THINKING.

IT WAS JUST A MATTER OF TIME

KEY BRAND DIMENSIONS OF BRAND VALUE

We already know brands and people interact in space and time, and that these interactions lead to brand value and can inform brand strategy and branding efforts. Time is a primary dimension. In the real world, people interact in space and time together, but for this chapter we explore a fictional universe where time operates in isolation. Specifically, we'll explore three critical dimensions of people's interactions with a brand: (1) First Moment with a brand; (2) Mass of Time with a brand; and (3) Velocity of Time.

Albert Einstein used thought experiments to derive his famous equation, $E = mc^2$, the paradigm-shifting relationship between mass and energy in the physical world and a foundation of his theory of relativity. Our interest is to similarly explore the relationship between people's accumulated mass of experiences with a brand and the resultant brand energy. We'll explore the concept of brand energy within a person and as a mysterious connective social force within a community. We'll also examine the power of established brands with large spatial footprints created from a mass of accumulated experiences in time, and we'll explore brands growing exponentially in this age of the Internet and global distribution systems.

As a thought, consider using different types of equations to explain how past experiences with a brand relate to brand energy. You are encouraged to open your imagination and think conceptually about how brands move through time and space. We are on a common journey across time through the words and visuals in this book.

TIME DIMENSIONS MODEL

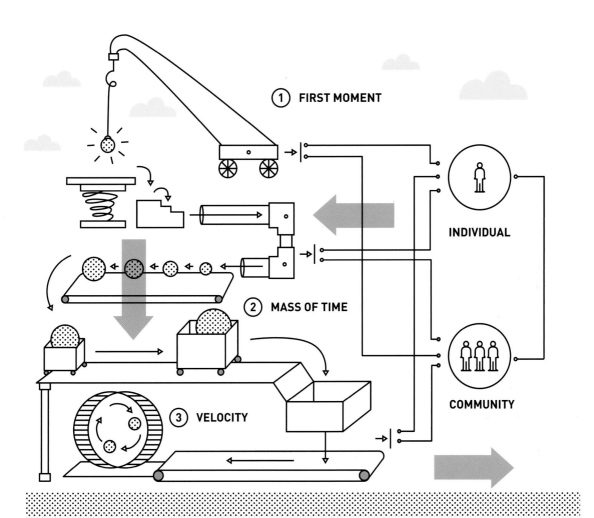

1 FIRST MOMENT

2 MASS OF TIME

3 VELOCITY

INDIVIDUAL

COMMUNITY

TWENTY-EIGHT MILLION BRAND MOMENTS

MOMENTS IN TIME

Time is both real and perceived. Today we have a wristwatch and an atomic clock to measure real time precisely. We also know perceived time speeds up and slows down. If this is news to you, compare an hour in Physics class to an hour with all your best friends and a barrel of beer. Or better yet, compare an hour walking around Stonehenge to an hour watching a 200-year-old clock tick.

When time becomes memorable, it turns into a moment. Experiences that are emotional, social, and multisensory increase the likelihood of becoming a moment. The first time someone tries a brand is a critical moment. We recall moments in time, not clock time, and many moments across clock time lead to long-term memory and habits. The good thing is, moments can be designed.

Historically, time was measured by full moons, a sundial, and the distance an average human could travel across geographic space, by foot, on earth. Going back into the history of time, we discover "moments" as a medieval unit of time with forty moments making a solar hour (as measured by a sundial). In modern measurements, this is approximately ninety seconds. Hence, a brand moment could be seen as ninety seconds long. Do the math using a typical eighty-year lifetime and you've got over 28 million brand-moment opportunities with each human on the planet. Let's get started.

OUR BRAND WAS FOUNDED BEFORE TIME

FIRST MOMENT

Every person with any memory of a brand has had a first brand moment. Although they may have had brand signals projected at them prior to that time, the first moment marks the first focus of attention and the formation of their first conscious brand memory. Groups of people might have similar, parallel histories with a brand, as well as interactions with each other that include the brand. As the years progress, new generations will be born and form their own first moments. Some will adopt brands that were introduced to them by their parents, carrying on the legacy of a family's brand usage. Some will just respect and admire a brand that was launched to people who are long since gone—people who had their own first moments and carried the brand's energy forward into the world in which it resides today.

Brands have long used age as a standard marker for quality; it conveys the "we've been around for a long time so you should trust us" message. Most people associate this with the cultural norm of trusting your elders. After all, they know best. While some of this belief system was crushed by the social rebellion of the 1960s, it still remains important to those who have raised their own children to respect age and experience.

In some industries, too much history can make a brand "uncool," using a term that itself has too much history. This is likely why you never hear Facebook, Google, or Microsoft use a founded date as a marker for quality. Though, in general, history means that a "heritage brand" has survived and connected with a loyal customer, delivering a valuable offer to our culture.

Veuve Clicquot is a 244-year-old brand of Champagne that looks rather sexy wrapped in potato fiber. It is made in the Champagne area of France, the only place where the name Champagne can be used legally. Clicquot goes far enough back in history to be the first to add red wine to produce a rosé Champagne. If that wasn't enough, in 1805, Veuve Clicquot became the first Champagne house to be run by a woman. The packaging is an example of how a 244-year-old brand can look nice in a new dress. So while the heritage offers trust, old brands can also be hip and luxurious.

In contrast and comparison, Mr. Jack Daniel's offers up a 141-year-old brand that makes Tennessee corn whiskey. The oldest American whiskey brand delivers trust through decades of consistently distilling and crafting whiskey. The brand has layers of meaning for many.

THOUGHT EXPERIMENT

HOW CAN BRANDS BECOME MORE HUMAN?

In fact, many people have a long-term relationship with the brand. If you take a tour in Lynchburg, Tennessee, you'll be treated to a nuanced history, but not a taste of the spirit (unless you head over the county line). And if you're fortunate enough, you'll be offered a square-inch plot of land and the option to become a Tennessee Squire Association member. New brands can't touch this legacy.

History brings meaning to a brand. And similar to a person, the more depth of meaning, the more interesting the individual. Consider how meaningful of a conversation you can have with an average teenager compared to a World War II veteran or tenured professor. Mr. Daniel's and Ms. Clicquot are certainly interesting individuals to bring into your life, as long as you do so responsibly!

Of course, since no one alive today was around for the launch of either of these brands, the brand energy is carried down through generations of people who share stories—stories that blur into legends. For brands like these, these legends were likely burned into our collective memories with a force that will last many lifetimes, particularly if refreshed with a sniff or a sip every so often.

RIDING BEAMS OF LIGHT

MASS OF TIME

It turns out that space and time are essentially different expressions of the same system. Gather enough physical mass to form a black hole and time nears to a stop. We'd stretch physics beyond credibility if we made direct connections between Einstein's discoveries and the world of brands, but we do know there is a connection between the mass and energy of brands.

A thought experiment about a bicycle changed the course of physics. In 1895, sixteen-year-old Albert Einstein wondered what would happen if he could ride his bike on a beam of light. The question dominated Einstein's thoughts, and in 1905 he published three papers that changed our world, leading to nuclear power plants, semiconductors, and GPS.

Heritage brands provide insight into the relationship between brands and mass. When we look at the top brands in packaged foods, the top sellers have been around for decades. Think Heinz Ketchup, Morton Salt, and Kraft Macaroni & Cheese. These brands have huge and well-established physical footprints in grocery stores—

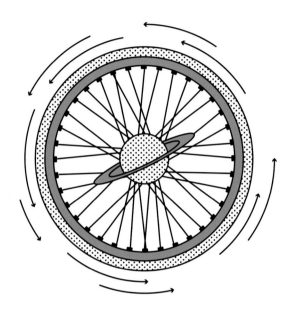

and their longevity has planted neural networks in the collective consciousness. Flanker brands, Annie's Macaroni & Cheese, Diamond Crystal Salt, and Hunt's Ketchup, nibble around the edges, but the big packaged-food brands tend to stay big.

Concurrently, Internet technologies are now dethroning brands and entire industries because brands can move at the speed of light. Today 39 percent of all revenue in the giant marketing conglomerates (WPP, Interpublic, Omnicom, Publicis) is from digital services. Advertising used to dominate this game. Now Amazon, Slack, Airbnb, Etsy, and other Silicon Valley darlings are eating the lunch of dozens of established industries. These modern Internet brands are using the speed of the Internet to accumulate mass quickly.

At the same time, speed cannot optimize real-world production and distribution systems that take decades to establish. Nor can speed establish the trillions of neural connections that legacy brands have established. What is certain, though, is that speed is a functional cousin of mass, and legacy brands are at risk more now than ever before. Legacy brands are particularly vulnerable to fast brands because the big brands cannot re-engineer and rebrand themselves quickly. Mass has advantages and problems. Woe to the complacent.

Engagement is increasingly seen as being more important than mass-media impressions in this brave, new brand world. Time-based metrics are now more common for brand managers, replacing older metrics such as impressions, reach, and frequency. Emotional, full-sensory moments are more important than raw mass of time spent with a brand. Time spent with a brand is a rough proxy for engagement, but a deeper dive into this underwater cave will lead to the moments designed to engage.

THIS MOMENT ISN'T OUR MOMENT

DRAMATIC MOMENTS

The moments people experience during their interactions with a brand may include dramatic times in its history. While these are not the type of moments we reference throughout this book, they are important in the history of the brand and our relationship with them as people. These "moments in time" may include dates when a brand was sold, divested, upgraded, turned around, or repositioned entirely for a new market. Kodak, the brand of film and cameras known to have once owned an entire industry of film, provides a timely example.

Founded in 1888 by George Eastman, a profound thinker by any contemporary standard, Kodak, at its peak in 1976, owned 90 percent of film sales and 80 percent of cameras in the U.S. market. Another key date is 1975, when Kodak developed the first digital camera, but sat on it for fears of infringing on existing film sales. Then in 1984, Kodak passed on the Olympic sponsorship and allowed Fuji an open door into the U.S.

market. And in 2013, the company re-emerged from bankruptcy after selling off half a billion dollars in intellectual property to take a fresh look at a bright and colorful (likely more digital) future.

These dates are hard to see when you're right in the middle of them, but they focus on the decisions and moments when the brand makes dramatic shifts. Similar to the stock market having single-day dramatic moves, these are singular days in the history of a brand's life. If you follow the thinking that a brand's energy resides in people's collective memories, Kodak suffered a heart attack and its new owners had some lifestyle choices to make. No more steak for the Kodak brand, but with some innovative changes, it is making a comeback in digital printing, graphics, and film for Hollywood. Life's theater can have a fourth and fifth act.

PROMOTION AT THE SPEED OF LIGHT

MAD MEN 2.0

Mass media and mass advertising are slowly becoming micro. Someday many of these legacy media systems may die quickly. The millennial generation is essentially opting out of mass media, and demography becomes destiny. Hot new media sources today include Vice, BuzzFeed, Medium, Digg, Reddit, and YouTube. Whether these channels will become dominant is beside the point. What is clear is that the Internet is bulldozing traditional mass-media models.

As an illustration, consider the subservient chicken by Burger King. If you don't know this character, it was concocted by twisted minds at Crispin Porter + Bogusky (CP+B) to promote the idea of having "chicken" your way. A man in a tattered chicken suit stood in a room with a couch, and when you typed a command he would comply. Anything too close to a rated-R request was returned with a shameful look, but otherwise, almost any command you could consider, the chicken would do.

The result was a gargantuan number of hours

A GREEK GOD NAMED JACOB

A COLLEAGUE IS EATING YOGURT AT HIS DESK, BUT YOU DON'T RECOGNIZE THE BRAND. TWO DAYS PASS AND A GIRLFRIEND OFFERS YOU A GREEK YOGURT AND YOU TRY IT. A WEEK PASSES AND YOU SEE GREEK YOGURT AT THE GROCERY STORE AND BUY A FEW FOR YOUR DAUGHTER WHO'S HOME FROM COLLEGE. THE NEXT TIME YOUR DAUGHTER SEES YOU AT YOUR LOCAL COFFEE SHOP WITH FRIENDS SHE THANKS YOU IN FRONT OF ALL YOUR GIRLFRIENDS. "THANK YOU FOR BUYING CHOBANI, MOM. IT'S MY FAVE. LOVE YOU SO MUCH." MOM FEELS LIKE A GODDESS. YES, YOGURT HAS ALWAYS HAD PERCEIVED AND REAL HEALTH BENEFITS, BUT NOW A NEW EXOTIC "GREEK GOD" VARIATION DOUBLES THE PROTEIN AND HALVES THE SUGAR. THIS BRAND HAS JUST EARNED A PLACE IN YOUR LONG-TERM MEMORY AND VALUE FOR SHAREHOLDERS WILLING TO TAKE A RISK ON HAMDI ULUKAYA, THE TURKISH IMMIGRANT. THANK YOU HAMDI FOR INSPIRING A SIMPLIFIED EXAMPLE OF OUR JACOB'S LADDER MODEL.

playing with this goofy bird. This was a designed moment in time, for the entertainment of the average Joe to build an online brand for a creepy character owned by Burger King. Just considering mass of time, this was a huge contribution to the Burger King brand, and was culturally relevant for approximately three years. Unfortunately for Burger King, this was a one-act play. They were unable to engage their newfound audience in a continuing dialogue. The heat gained by this effort has dissipated and the brand has returned to struggling in a highly competitive category, with significant drag from a fractious franchise system. Enduring mass comes from increasing product usage through a superior experience. Stunts buy engagement time, but are hard to sustain. For something more sustainable, let's turn to the Chipotle experience.

Chipotle Cultivate festivals are extravaganzas involving popular national acts, local chefs, and local food and culture in select cities. They are hitting culturally vibrant cities, places where the heat dissipated from the events will travel the greatest distance throughout social media. Chipotle is essentially inviting influential cultural creatives to a party. These immersive, day-long events tastefully incorporate Chipotle's food and criticism of big fast-food brands into communal, multisensory love fests filled to the edge of the burrito bowl with moments.

We see this as an example of a brand like Chipotle designing a sustainable model of brand engagement that accumulates mass of sensory interaction for long periods, creating memorable moments. Chipotle Cultivate is the modern and elegant version of restaurant micro-advertising. As you'll discover later in our Jacob's Ladder model, the Chipotle experience is designed to form strong memories, since it involves time, multiple senses, community (social), and emotions. Compare the power of this day-long experience with three impressions from a ten-second TV spot to promote the brand. It's like comparing tacos and dim sum.

CAN YOU FEEL THE MOVEMENT?

VELOCITY OF INTERACTIONS

We are drawn to fast-moving objects as they move through time and diffuse new knowledge and habits along the way. Fast-moving brands find it easier to gain attention, interest, desire, trial use, and buzz. Words and actions spread. And this buzz is rarely, if ever, manufactured by clever TV commercials: It originates from user experience. Given the horrific failure rate of new-product launches, savvy product developers aim for a 10-times improvement in performance over existing options (e.g., Spotify, Uber, Costco, Cedar Point Amusement Park). The best new offerings are designed to be highly engaging, educational, and valuable from day one. With innovations this large, you'd almost be a fool not to try the competing offering. And once bought, twice sold. In these cases, branding and marketing communication is charged with increasing adoption to reach profitable scale faster.

If this momentum is maintained, new branded products can rapidly unseat entrenched offerings in established categories. This is particularly true in the age of the social Internet. A typical path for a flanker brand is to enter at the low end and rapidly move upward. Apple is unique in that they moved in at the high end and have started to move slightly down-market, creating a new category of luxury electronics.

This is where gargantuan data scales exponentially and we start to see the importance of understanding fractals, memes, and diffusion in the world of brands. If your brand is small enough and you have a finger on the pulse of activity, you can have an intuitive sense of brand velocity. It can be described as the calm before the storm or the water rushing past your ankles as you face an ocean wave twice your height. New innovations move across time in unique ways.

Once a brand hits scale, the velocity of time interactions becomes more challenging to measure. Sophisticated big-data analytics can answer significant questions for brand owners and their collaborators. One brand that likely has good data on these interactions over time is Google, a brand made out of designs, data, computers, and algorithms. It sure would be fun to peek behind that curtain.

A mass retailer like Target already uses big data to better understand shopper behaviors and predict what offers to make to households. So when you buy a typical basket of items, they can offer something you will likely need based on past purchases of other shoppers. A surprising illustration used by the *New York Times* was a family with a teenage daughter getting an offer for pregnancy vitamins before the father was aware of his young daughter's status. As a customer, this might make you angry, but if you look down from the clouds you can see a world in which you get discount offers for things you didn't realize you needed, but you do, and it could be a pleasant surprise. As a brand owner, this may give you the energy of a quadruple espresso.

QUADRUPLE THE FUN OF AN ESPRESSO

VELOCITY AND ENERGY

The touchstone book on how new innovations spread is Everett Rogers's *The Diffusion of*

Innovations, first published in 1962. Mr. Rogers identifies five elements of rapid new-product adoption: (1) Innovation; (2) Adopters; (3) Diffusion; (4) Time; (5) Social Systems. Innovation is the physical product, service, meme, or brand that is new and seeking social adoption. Adopters are people and organizations that live inside of broader communities. Diffusion is the process of transferring information, actions, and energy between adopters. Time is the passage of time or perceived time as the diffusion spreads. And last, the Social System is about the external influences of communication along with the internal influences of social communities and opinion leaders. This model is important because successful brands are typically tied to innovation.

Silicon Valley knows a thing or two about how new innovations move across time as well, and they have demonstrated an appetite for paying top dollar for fast-moving brands—$22 billion for WhatsApp, as an example. San Francisco denizen Geoffrey Moore created a model to classify adopters of technology into innovators, early adopters, early majority, late majority, and laggards. East Coast genius and now Google futurist Ray Kurzweil added to the art and science of technological prediction by plotting out the growth curves of multiple technologies and then imagining what could happen in future inflection points. Kurzweil predicted the rise of local area networks and then the Internet; now he projects affordable computers as smart as humans are just around the corner.

When our colleague Jeffry Brown worked to project future opportunities for Steve Jobs in the 1980s, they used Rogers's model and other diffusion models to project the introduction of Apple smartphones and tablets by the late 1990s. The board thought Jobs, Jeff, and their team were dreaming beyond reality. The projections may have been a few years off, but Jobs and company were far from crazy. As a bunch of smart people have said, "Prediction is very difficult, especially if it's about the future."

Rapid acceptance of technological innovations is critically important to new brands, and increasingly important to established brands.

New and improved always helps. To help us understand brand diffusion, let's quickly review our models showing how brands move across time and space as described in Chapter 1. Our Time Dimensions model identifies how brands move across time: First Moment > Mass of Time > Velocity of Time. Our Space Dimensions model shows how Brand Owners work with Brand Handlers to influence Communities and People. Signals within both space and time dimensions travel up our Jacob's Ladder model, or Signals > Senses > Moments > Memories > Energy > Sales > Profits > Value. Our models provide a new systems theory of brand diffusion that can be used to create questions and generate ideas to improve branding and estimated brand value.

High-velocity disruptions are showing up everywhere these days, and not just in the digital world. If this seems like an exaggeration, consider a certain four-year-old fashion brand that has taken on the marketing machine of Procter & Gamble, founded in 1837. P&G is the parent brand to Pampers and a variety of other brands focused on Mom and her family. Which brand is currently valued at $1 billion and growing in P&G's bread-and-butter categories? The answer is The Honest Company. If you haven't heard of The Honest Company, go to *www.honest.com*. Founders Jessica Alba, Brian Lee, Christopher Gavigan, and Sean Kane are poster children for brand velocity and how it translates into brand energy.

Of course, it's easy to point to fast-moving brands and think that this is easy to do. What we do know is that time engagement is a rough proxy for the energy of brands, and that a rapid increase in time spent with a brand means something good is happening. Time is a precious resource, after all. You can make more money, but not more time. The decision to spend time happens inside the hearts and minds of people, which we'll explore in the following case study.

THOUGHT EXPERIMENT

HOW WOULD A MARKETING TEAM'S BONUSES WORK IF YOU COULD RELIABLY MEASURE BRAND VALUE ON AN ANNUAL SCHEDULE?

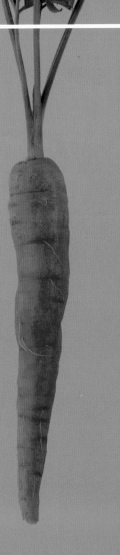

WHY WHEATIES ARE MADE OF GOLD

GENERAL MILLS CASE STUDY

Theory is fascinating for academia, but the real world is where real learning happens. And the best way to test a brilliant concept is to put it out into the real world, unprotected. We're going to explore the case of Wheaties, which bulldozed its way into the once uncluttered markets of breakfast cereals and pioneered advertising on radio and TV at the most opportune time.

Let's go way back to the 1923 creation of the brand that would have been Washburn's Gold Medal Whole Wheat Flakes. Fortunately, the name was shortened to Wheaties by the company we now call General Mills. In 1926, Wheaties aired the first ever singing radio commercial, using the jingle "Have you tried Wheaties?" The next year began Wheaties' first baseball sponsorship and the introduction of the slogan "Breakfast of Champions." During the Great Depression, Wheaties became a household name with product testimonials by Lou Gehrig and other famous athletes. In 1933, it introduced Iowan Ronald Reagan to Hollywood, and, in 1939, it was one of four brands featured in the first TV commercials as an experiment by the Federal Communications Commission during a baseball broadcast. This is what is known as good timing. Wheaties had rapid velocity of time interactions and rapid diffusion, and today they have tremendous mass in the breakfast cereal category. Wheaties literally grew up with the growth of mass media.

In 1941, Wheaties was joined by Cheerios and other cereals, which later came to be known as the Big G Cereals. The original Cheerios inspired seemingly endless varieties, including the number one breakfast cereal sold today, Honey Nut Cheerios. As of August 2014, Honey Nut and the original Cheerios were in the first and fourth spots, respectively, of IRI's U.S. top ten bestselling cereal brands. Cheerios has long been a favorite of children, particularly as a take-along snack for busy moms with toddlers. Cheerios has a history of designing branded bowls and packages intended to facilitate these early first moments in many people's lives. Likewise, since it's not only a children's cereal, early Cheerios habits have led to a mass of time with the brand for a large portion of the population.

Wheaties is still a strong brand, but has faced headwinds during the past decade with offshoots that did not do well and the high cost of gracing its orange box with professional athletes. To help it change course, General Mills polled customers for their choice of extreme sport athletes outside major sporting franchises. This allowed it to both connect with millennial customers and save money when it signed on Anthony Pettis, the UFC lightweight champion, for its newly featured athlete.

REMEMBER YOUR FIRST TIME? CERTAINLY!

CONCLUDING MEMORIES

TIME PASSES QUICKLY, SPRINKLING THE RESIDUE OF EXPERIENCES AND MEMORIES. IF YOUR FIRST THOUGHT IS, "HOW CAN WE GET PEOPLE TO SPEND MORE TIME WITH OUR BRAND," YOU'RE HEADING IN THE RIGHT DIRECTION, SO LONG AS THAT TIME IS PLEASANT AND SOLVES PROBLEMS. HERE ARE SOME SUMMARIZING BITS TO ENJOY BEFORE THE NEXT LEAP FORWARD:

1. The first exposure to a brand can turn into a memorable moment if the experience is designed to be multisensory and emotionally compelling. More memorable moments over time will strengthen the memory of the brand.

2. Most brands can benefit from the amount of time in the market, yet only some should emphasize their founding date. Others should focus on innovation and being relevant in the present day, essentially de-emphasizing the founding date.

3. As habits form, people will spend a greater mass of time with the brand and develop purchasing habits. These habits can be hard for a challenger brand. This mass of time should be a voluntary engagement with the brand—a sign of brand health.

4. Fast-moving, high-velocity brands can unseat entrenched competitors if they can offer dramatic innovations in their offering and the way they go to market. The Internet and other technologies are making it easier for high-velocity challenger brands to disrupt entrenched brands with great mass of time.

5. High-velocity brands follow predictable paths of diffusion, although luck and timing play an important role in their success.

03

SPACE + BRANDS

NOW WE DIVE INTO THE THICK OF SPACE, BUT WE'LL REMAIN SAFE INSIDE CAPSULES OF EXISTING KNOWLEDGE ON BONDING HORMONES, APERTURES OF TRUST, AND SCALES TO MEASURE FAME. IF YOU FEEL LIKE YOU'VE TAKEN A HIT ON THE HEAD, THAT'S GOOD, BECAUSE OUR VERY THOUGHTS CANNOT EXIST WITHOUT THE PHYSICAL. CHEMICAL DEPENDENCIES WILL BE EXPOSED, ALONG WITH OUR MISTRUST OF GRANDMA WHEN SHE WEARS LEATHER PANTS. IF THIS ISN'T ENOUGH TO PIQUE YOUR CURIOSITY, BE READY TO EXPLORE SYNCHRONICITY (WITHOUT THE POLICE) AND WILLIE NELSON'S FRIENDSHIP WITH SNOOP DOGG. FINALLY, WE GET A LITTLE TOUCHY WITH DESIGNED MOMENTS, AND IF YOU THINK SOCIAL IS A DIGITAL THING, WE'VE GOT WORDS TO EXCHANGE. IF THIS ISN'T PHYSICAL ENOUGH, CONSIDER TAKING UP KICKBOXING. ENJOY EXPLORING BRANDS IN SPACE.

BRANDS IN SPACE

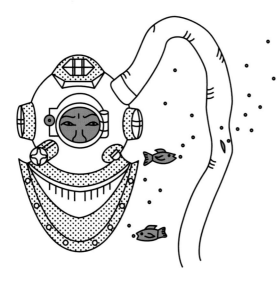

Now we dive deep into what happens when bodies and brands meet in space. It's easy to forget about our bodies as we ponder yesterday or try to imagine how we'll get everything done tomorrow. But if you take a few deep breaths, you'll start to feel this container of consciousness that navigates you through time. Sometimes your body will come across brands through brand handlers—online, through mass media, in retailers, or just out there as you travel around. Brands are always perceived through the body.

You will also notice there are other people around you—family, friends, colleagues—and their opinions of brands will matter more than you know. People in communities you affiliate with use brands you recognize and sometimes you will talk with them about brands. Sometimes you'll meet people who represent the brands directly, such as service people in restaurants and retailers. Self-identity is built through relationships with others.

Brand perceptions are filtered through your senses directly or indirectly through the opinions of others. When brands and people meet in space, it's a very social and sensual experience, as you will see.

SOCIAL IS A CHEMICAL THING

YOU CAN'T LIVE WITHOUT IT

People have experiences across time, but we can't do it without bodies in space. Three things pulled us out of the primordial ooze: thumbs, our brain capacity, and our social abilities. It's a bit of a simplification, but the point to be made is that social relations defined human beings long before Facebook, Twitter, and other social media platforms. Social is a reflex. It is impossible to remove social thoughts from your brain. Social is a muscle we relax and flex and relax and flex, consciously and subconsciously, all day long.

From the moment a baby stares into mom's eyes, the social fixation begins. Babies must bond with their parents to survive (having big eyes and being cute and cuddly helps). Drugs are also part of the picture. Oxytocin in particular seems to be an all-purpose hormone to bond mates, moms with babies, and friends. Studies have shown that trust is increased with higher levels of oxytocin. There are a number of ways to release oxytocin, but the most common is human-to-human touch. A good conversation may do it as well.

Research shows that the presence of oxytocin makes people more open to brands. And it is obvious brands seek this chemical connection. Witness the prevalence of big-eyed puppies, kitties, and babies in TV commercials, and consider the enduring power of Mickey Mouse, Thomas the Tank Engine, and My Little Pony. Chemically bonding your brand with your audiences is certainly an interesting objective to list in your next creative brief.

Big, oversized eyes dominate children's cartoon characters, and there is a reason why. When you hear, "The eyes are the window to the soul," it's not just a saying. The aperture of our pupils is a good signal to how receptive we are to a person, product, place, or thing. And we tend to mirror the eyes of people around us. Open your pupils and others may quickly follow suit.

ZUCK AND A BUCKET OF CHICKEN

WE ARE SOCIAL

Mark Zuckerberg is a poster child for the power of social. Facebook currently has more than 1.5 billion members globally, all sharing family photos, thumb icons, heartfelt memes, or perhaps the latest political news. People live for Facebook likes, because, well, everyone wants to be liked. What's amazing is that nobody is ever face-to-face on Facebook, yet our emotions react as if people were right there in front of us. And this entire online social revolution happened in just seven years.

Compare Zuck of Facebook with Colonel Sanders, founder of Kentucky Fried Chicken, who created a social innovation in 1957—the bucket of chicken. Families would buy a bucket of "finger lickin' good" chicken, bring it home, and dig into the intensely communal activity of sharing a meal together, all out of one common bucket. Perhaps the TV was on in the background in the early years, and today teens are probably smearing cooking oil on smartphones to avoid prying questions from the parents. The KFC bucket is still an enduring human, face-to-face social innovation. Fifty-five years later, there are more than 18,000 restaurants around the world. Meanwhile Facebook, the new kid on the block, is valued at more than twenty times the value of KFC. Behold the power of social, in our imagination, and in the real world.

Here's another social thought. Snoop Dogg was interviewed about his prodigious marijuana-smoking abilities and asked if there is anyone who could smoke as much. He said there was someone—Willie Nelson. Apparently Willie and Snoop are good friends, and on one adventure they went to Amsterdam to enjoy their shared hobby. Snoop relayed that they had a conversation about their skills, in a parking lot, behind a KFC, sharing a bucket of chicken. Who wouldn't have liked to run across that scene and post the photo on Facebook?

A THREESOME WITH MR. IVE

INDIVIDUAL UTILITY VS. SOCIAL UTILITY

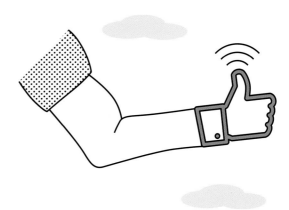

When you buy a watch, the expected utility value is telling time and perhaps the date. Add a brand name and you get a status symbol with social utility value that could attract mates or business associates. When Apple first introduced the iPhone, it became common for people to put them on the table during meetings or a meal, right next to a glass of water that could destroy an $800 iPhone. Jonathan Ive designed a device with two forms of social utility: being digitally connected to others anywhere and anytime, and being socially ranked in the physical world. Now, consider how many millions of iPhones took their last breath at the bottom of a toilet just after its last Tweet. The power of social knows no boundaries.

Society and the individual are in frequent conflict. We need others to fulfill ourselves, but we are, in our natural state, rather selfish. Society puts so much pressure on us to portray our status positively, yet when we are most comfortable is at home with people who couldn't care less about our status (well, they still care, just less than the broader society).

You can hear it in language. Consider this statement from a casual conversation between one of the authors and a friend: "We finally broke down and bought a Tesla." Was this individual peer pressured to buy an $80,000 vehicle in order to fit into a social circle? Is this equal to the

THOUGHT EXPERIMENT

DOES THE COUNTER-REVOLUTION OF SNAPCHAT AND A PUSH FOR PSEUDO-PRIVACY REPRESENT A CULTURAL SHIFT IN THE NEXT GENERATION? IS THE NEXT GENERATION GOING AS FAR AS HIDING FROM BRANDS?

high-school pressure to smoke a cigarette out by the fence lining school property?

When we buckle to pressure we might find ourselves out of balance with our own values, yet feeling more connected to our social circles. This conflict is constant and in some cases debilitating. We pay a tax to fit into a group, either sacrificing our values or making a car payment for a vehicle we perhaps didn't need. And while our social circles have been influencing us since we wrote on cave walls, the modern social mediums have certainly amplified social pressures.

The social mediums we have today amplify social anxiety already present in our culture. Your friends dump buckets of ice over their head for charity and post it on Facebook, so you want to do it, too. Social media has handed an overflowing gas can and match to everyone with a computer or smartphone. But when we balance this digital world with our physical world, we are more likely to trust someone we've shared a meal or a cup of coffee with. Which leads us back to trust.

GONE SHOPPING FOR LEATHERS WITH GRANDMA

THE APERTURE OF TRUST

Your roommate the rocker just finishing college went shopping for leather pants, with her grandmother. She left a note on the fridge. Do you question whether she's been kidnapped and left this note as an obvious signal? Most people trust Grandma, but shopping for leather pants? Context makes all the difference. We are more likely to trust people who are closer in physical proximity, age, demographic profile, beauty, and similar social status. Just as our eyes mirror how we feel about people we talk to—our pupils dilating or constricting, depending on the level of trust—we open or close ourselves to advice depending on how much we trust the source and the situation.

Celebrities have traditionally been important when it comes to fashion and style. Our aspiring rocker is more likely to look for social signals online in something like *Rock Revolt Magazine*

than on a shopping trip to the mall with Grandma. And leather pants mentioned in an article in a magazine she trusts will carry more weight than something pushed by a rocker in an ad. She's also likely to search around online for reviews and pricing. Perhaps she'll end up ordering Sexy Faux Leather High-Waist Leggings for $7.88 instead of a $200 pair of chaps, particularly since there are 588 reviews with an average of four stars on Amazon. Free shipping included.

Reading these previous paragraphs, it's hard to consider how quickly we judge the signals we are being sent. We compare trust to a camera aperture: The speed with which it changes is hard to measure or even observe in real life. We have outlined four dimensions of space, starting with the brand owner to brand handlers to your community to yourself. We have degrees of trust for each of these dimensions. We wander through our days making subconscious micro-judgments about whether we'd trust the source of a signal.

While our college student would likely proclaim unbreakable trust in Grandma, further conversation about leather leggings would reveal this to be an idealist lie. As people, we believe that trust is as black and white as a light switch in a coal mine: We either do or don't trust a brand or someone. Yet, in fact, trust is more contextual and contains more shades of gray than Pantone Inc. could imagine. This perspective helps us respect the profound complexity for a brand owner to orchestrate a message, messenger, and medium in space and time.

FAME IS MERELY A SCALE THING

OUR ROLE IN SOCIETY

Andy Warhol said, "In the future, everyone will be world-famous for 15 minutes." This quote was once mildly absurd, but it's feasible now, at least within communities of interest. Fame is both wholesale and retail now, and is, because of smartphones, within everybody's reach.

For example, take Miranda Sings (a.k.a. Colleen Ballinger Evans), a YouTube star who entertains tween and teen girls with cornball humor and slapstick comedy. She has more than 5 million YouTube subscribers, and her videos regularly have more than 1 million views. She performs in sold-out shows and, of course, has a self-help book, *Selp-Helf*. Most likely, you have never heard of Miranda, but for young girls, she can be an obsession. These days there are thousands of Miranda-like people out there on the Internet and even more wannabes and trolls who leave hate notes. Take Wit & Delight as an elegant example, started by Kate Arends in 2009. It has 2.6 million followers on Pinterest. She is humble about her success and attributes only her uncompromising intentions and aesthetic to her fame as a content curator. Fame is no longer an

FIFTEEN MINUTES WITH ANDY

ANDY WARHOL STARTED HIS RISE TO FAME BY ILLUSTRATING CAMPBELL'S SOUP CANS AND ASKING, "WHAT IS ART?" IN 2004, THE CAMPBELL SOUP COMPANY PAID THE ANDY WARHOL FOUNDATION TO RUN A LIMITED PROMOTION USING THE ANDY WARHOL VERSION OF THEIR CANS. THE CANS ARE SO COVETED THAT THE COMPANY STILL FIELDS CALLS ASKING FOR THE CANS. DOES ANYONE ELSE SEE THE IRONY BAKED INTO THAT ONE? THE MOST RECENT CAMPBELL'S PAINTING WENT ON SALE FOR $11.8 MILLION. LIKELY CAMPBELL'S DOESN'T SEE A PENNY OF THAT SALE, BUT ANDY SHOWERED CAMPBELL'S WITH PLENTY OF FAME, AND HE BELIEVED WE'D ALL GET OUR FIFTEEN MINUTES OVER TIME. BY OUR CALCULATIONS, IT WOULD TAKE 13,652 YEARS FOR EACH U.S. CITIZEN TO ENJOY FIFTEEN MINUTES OF BROADCAST FAME. MOST OF US WOULD BE BETTER OFF JUST WEARING A T-SHIRT THAT READS "I'M A LEGEND IN MY OWN MIND."

all-or-nothing proposition. A whole generation of kids are throwing away the TV remote and tuning in to YouTube, and likely many of them will take a shot at their fifteen minutes of fame.

We have found Mr. Warhol's quote to be a work of art in itself, open to interpretations and considerations. But maybe that's because we're word geeks. What is certain is that many claim this quote truly came of age with the birth of the Internet and social media. Many people have seen their fifteen minutes come and go, with reality television certainly accelerating this flywheel. Yet, every person in the United States having fifteen minutes of fame would require some significant broadcast time and bandwidth.

Yet, perhaps what Andy meant and what we are seeing come true today is a scale of fame he was referencing. Have you ever heard of someone referred to as "famous" in the industry or a person given the compliment of "you're famous" in our gaggle? This flies in contrast with the traditional view on fame, which is a mass population of Middle Americans who enjoyed a particular movie, album, or television show. Now, we have famous business leaders, Internet publishers, Pinterest "pinners," Twitter socialites, and a variety of others.

Perhaps our interpretation of Andy's work of art in words could be that we achieve a level of fame in one or many of our communities. For instance, we have a friend—formerly of General Mills—who identified a flaw in Lucky Charms Cereal: The cereal did not contain an actual charm in the mix of marshmallows. It was remedied and this individual has this notable moment attached to his name in the legends and lore of General Mills. This may not be the fame he was seeking, but it gets attached to him still the same.

The other definition for fame could be an individual who is known and admired by people who the individual does not know even exist. If that's the case, then most high-school cheerleaders achieve this fame before graduation. Whatever the case, the larger form of fame can change a person from behaving like a human being to behaving like a corporation. This is when the individual becomes a brand handler, pitching products and endorsing brands, and is no longer part of our community. When they act more like a person—tweeting, instagramming, etc.,—we are more likely to see their human side and our aperture of trust will open up again.

Let's get technical with fame and conclude with a protein shake of intellectual content. Scale-free degree distribution (SFDD) is your next favorite acronym to drop in a meeting to see if anyone gets it. "What's the potential for SFDD on that idea?" may win new friends or fire up some frenemies. These are environments, made possible by the world widening web, where a celebrity (hub) can exist within a network and create a power law distribution of connections. This distribution curve favors the highly influential hubs within the network and then has a long tail of less connected nodes.

"What the frack does this mean for your brand?" you may ask. Potentially many things, but in short, fame is a matter of being the node that is well connected within a hub of influence. And if you want to scale awareness, finding the hubs of influence is a good place to start. Social media and the Internet are liquid spaces for memes and fame to spread, even if it is for a short time. Brands can catch free rides if they find the right meme or, better, hitch a ride on a large movement.

BEING SOCIAL ISN'T BEING DIGITAL

THE SEARCH FOR SOCIAL PERFECTION

Take a deep dive into the world of social and digital networks. Spend some time looking at how many people are active in each platform. What surrounds you starts to look like the entire universe, and could be so if you never left your futon for the office or a vacation. But rest assured there is a physical world out there. Our communities are also real. They do not just exist in a digital universe. Not only is social perfection unachievable, describing a real human social network in digital form has not yet been achieved.

This is likely because we are physical beings with more senses and sensibilities than the digital and social worlds can replicate. Yet, while online social networks are not human, they have structure and meaning relative to you as a person.

So sorry to alarm you here, but you have a disease, and yes it is contagious. You have homophily, and there's no prescription for getting rid of it. There isn't even a drug company working on it, at least we don't think so. It means you have a preference for people like you. It could be ethnicity, race, sex, age, religion, education, or a favorite video game. It's a subconscious bias.

People who think like you do can be categorized by profession (designers, accountants, lawyers, doctors, librarians) or other preferred social activities (snowboarders, bicyclists, entrepreneurs, hikers) or by beliefs and desires. You likely make similar decisions as these real-world and online imaginary friends. It doesn't make you a clone, even though some have made the argument that free will is a false hope (that is not our rabbit hole). You are heavily influenced by belief systems and biases, with the always-open option of making your own choices, and the Internet has significantly widened social options for individuals and brands.

ONE + ONE = THREE

WHAT MAKES US HUMAN

People are born into circumstances and opportunities. At our moment of birth we start having emotional reactions, forming beliefs, and having desires that inform our behaviors. Our interactions with other human beings define who we are, starting with that first bonding moment with Mom. Where we are born (the physical location) impacts our belief systems in profound ways. A baby born in New York City will be immersed in a "me" society, where the individual is more important than the community. A baby born in Beijing will grow up in a "we" society, with greater emphasis given to what's good for the whole versus the individual.

As you can imagine, a macro location has profound impact, but you can also dive all the way down to the impact of your birth zip code (for United States readers). Imagine being born into Douglas County, Omaha, Nebraska (68178), versus Westchester County, Purchase, New York (10577). How you speak, where you go to college, what you're income is likely to be, and the community you surround yourself with will likely be vastly different between these zip codes. Physical space has an impact on the individual at a macro and micro level. So if physical space matters, can we triangulate it with meaning and personality?

A JUNG EINSTEIN

ARCHETYPES, SYNCHRONICITY, AND LOCALITY

Lucky for us, Carl Jung and Albert Einstein had dinner once. Perhaps if they lived in the collaborative economy of today they would have jumped on Google Drive and copublished a document on synchronicity and quantum mechanics. Both were working on their own forms of a unified general theory. Neither succeeded, but Jung made some impressive insights into our collective inner noggins.

Jung saw that archetypes dominate the subconscious that informs our waking consciousness. Complexes formed around mother and father and community can weigh heavily upon people, or free them to do amazing things. Jung also saw that we run across situations of synchronicity, times when events seem to have deep personal meaning. Similarly, Einstein spent all of his later years trying to develop a theory of everything through physics. Many scientists and philosophers seem driven by the concept of meaning, and Jung believed that societies also search for a collective meaning. And no, we have not been hanging out with Snoop Dogg and Willie Nelson.

The idea of meaning connecting everything is helpful in a discussion of brands, because brands occupy space and time in our lives, so they also contain meaning. And, through interaction, socialization, and consumption, we transfer meaning between these ethereal objects known as brands. Brands take on a life of their own as symbols, beyond the people who start, manage, and sometimes accidentally devalue them. Brands become part of our collective consciousness.

Synchronicity attempts to explain events that seem to have no connection except through meaning derived from our collective subconscious. To take that idea forward to an era of truly large numbers—that's a classic term for big data—we can see synchronicity events as statistically possible outliers. Synchronicity can also be designed by brands and moments through the use of archetypes.

Carl Jung used archetypes to describe human personalities baked right into our subconscious. If you're unaware of archetypes because you slept through a Psych 101 class in college, here's how you can get up to speed in exactly thirty-five minutes. Read the Wikipedia on archetypes for five minutes. Watch a sitcom for thirty minutes and pick out the archetypal characters. Or if you're a late-blooming overachiever, watch any made-for-television Shakespeare play and do the same.

WOULD NIKOLA DRIVE A TESLA?

THE FOUNDERS OF TESLA MOTORS NAMED THEIR ENERGIZED BRAND AFTER NIKOLA TESLA (1856–1943), A SERBIAN AMERICAN PHYSICIST, ENGINEER, INVENTOR, AND PHILOSOPHER. THE BRAND OF TESLA HAS BROUGHT ELECTRIC VEHICLES INTO OUR MODERN TRANSPORTATION SYSTEM. THIS WASN'T DONE THROUGH THE TRADITIONAL DEALER NETWORKS DRAINING THE MARGINS OF THIS FLEDGLING BRAND. INSTEAD, THE BRAND WENT DIRECT THROUGH POP-UP RETAIL AND BY DELIVERING A TEST-DRIVE EXPERIENCE STARTING AT YOUR OWN DOORSTEP. THE EXPERIENCE IS DESIGNED TO BE MEMORABLE, ENGAGING, AND COVETED LONG AFTER IT HAS ENDED. THIS IS A DESIGNED EXPERIENCE, AND WHEN A DRIVER PRESSES THE PEDAL (NOT THE GAS) IN AN ELECTRIC CAR, A DESIGNED MOMENT IS REALIZED, AND AN ANGEL GETS ITS WINGS.

THOUGHT EXPERIMENT

IF A DRUG COMPANY HAD A PILL THAT REDUCED OUR TENDENCY TO BEFRIEND PEOPLE LIKE US (HOMOPHILY)—HOW WOULD THIS AFFECT RACE AND GENDER RELATIONS?

These same concepts can be applied to humanize brands, which is the subject of the great book *The Hero and the Outlaw*. The important element to grasp is that archetypes are born out of how we define ourselves as human beings. They are also used to describe brands and, better yet, used to define the behavior of brands.

Simple example: a typical healthcare organization embodies the category archetype of Caregiver. This makes sense even if you only understand the word *caregiver*. But what distinguishes that healthcare system from other systems is the secondary and tertiary archetypes, like Outlaw or perhaps Sage. The Sage makes sense, but requires a focus on recruiting the best minds in medicine. The Mayo Clinic in Rochester, Minnesota, is a great example of a healthcare system behaving like a Sage archetype. Now, when this same system folds in the Outlaw archetype, what does it mean? They are breaking some of the conventions of the healthcare category. Example: buying a block of downtown Minneapolis with a notorious history to insert a health clinic near a basketball and hotel complex in the party district. And then you ask yourself, who else has done such a thing? Don't struggle to find an example. Mayo does it, and stretched their Sage archetype into the Outlaw archetype. Amazing.

FROM WHENCE DESIGN CAME

DESIGNED MOMENTS GET TOUCHY

The broadest definition of design includes architecture, fashion, crafts, interiors, digital, textiles, graphics, industrial, and product. The bumbershoot to cover this span of disciplines has taken on greater meaning in our society over the last decade. Design has become a discipline at the strategic roundtable of business and industry. If this is news to you, look up the recent growth of the chief design officer title inside corporate brands like Pepsi, 3M, and P&G.

As design has taken the elevator up from the drawing board to the boardroom, we see a higher order of thinking forming. The most beautiful threads woven into all design disciplines include thoughtful process, empathy for the humans, and an intention to create engaging experiences. These three legs come together nicely under a stool that some refer to as experience design. And if memorable moments lead to designed experiences, we can extrapolate the highest discipline of design is a designer of moments.

We see a bright future for those who can connect the physical and digital worlds with ease. This new mind of the creative individual is not constrained by the old definition of "creative" or "designer," but can drop those two into a blender and press the purée button. This higher order of designer can facilitate how a brand interacts in space, by engaging as many senses as possible. They saunter to a digital universe and offer greater depth to social through a designed conversation. The design thinker of our next century is going to be given far greater opportunity and responsibility for the relationship between people and brands than the previous century. We've sewn responsibility with opportunity into the cushion of this throne intentionally.

According to AdAge.com, Target as a retailer, curator, and heat source for design has been providing the larger brand community with some worthy stories. Target took on design as a differentiator to the $475 billion gorilla known as Walmart just about two decades ago. But many in the design community, if pressed, would have said Target went an inch deep to merely use design as an aesthetic tool—essentially moving the beauty department up rather than moving design out of the department into the executive suite. Now, the stories coming from Target include redesigned children's utensils, camping products, and kitchen linens that are functionally smart and aesthetically pleasing. This elegant evolution in thinking came after a horrific data breach. There's nothing like a defibrillator to shock a corporate culture into a healthier way of looking at design.

Mark this page in your book and look back on Target in the next ten years. You'll witness the next decade's example of design thinking—Apple being our most recent—having a dramatic impact on the growth of a brand.

KINDNESS IS
CERTAINLY GOODNESS

THE PHYSICS OF KINDNESS

Let's explore the space dimensions with KIND Healthy Snacks and see where that takes us. KIND started in 2004 within the nutritional snack bar market space with KIND Bars. The growth in units sold, from 10 million in 2007 to 450 million in 2013—all within the time frame of one of the most devastating worldwide recessions in history. By 2014, its market share nearly doubled, from 4.6 percent in 2013 to nearly 9 percent in a category with 10 percent growth overall. So what makes KIND Healthy Snacks so special?

KIND is guided by a single vision: "Do the KIND thing." Founder Daniel Lubetzky manages his brand with a philosophy comparable to past great ones (Steve Jobs, Richard Branson, and Walt Disney). The company has soul and integrity and will not compromise on their values. They know who they are, what they make, and why, and remain highly principled and disciplined to this end.

Three simple anchors hold the brand in a good place: health, taste, and social responsibility. This is embodied in the company's slogan, "Being KIND to your body, KIND to your taste buds, and KIND to your world." This personalized message is an update of the original version, with "your" replacing "the" throughout. Details and nuances matter to a brand like KIND. Daniel states in his recent book *Do the KIND Thing*, "staying true to your brand is harder and more important than many realize. If you steer your brand in the wrong direction, or dilute the message, your customers may feel betrayed."

Fortune magazine noted in its February 2014 issue that "Kind also relies in part on Lubetzky's original mission—spreading kindness—to drive awareness of the product. Rather than rely strictly on direct sampling, company employees are now distributing plastic cards that are meant to reward random acts of kindness. If they see a person doing a kind act like giving up a seat on the subway or helping an elderly pedestrian across the street, they give the do-gooder the card. In turn, Kind will send the Samaritan a couple bars as well as another card to pay the kindness forward to someone else. The company, which calls itself 'not-only-for profit,' also has pledged thousands annually to support customer-generated projects that give back to the community."

Back in 2013, KIND had 300,000 card subscribers and estimated that 1 million people had been touched by acts of kindness inspired by KIND. In a June 2013 interview Lubetzky told AdvertisingAge, "The goal is to move from being a 'business that people like into being a state of mind and a community and a movement.'" While he attributed only 5 percent of the company's growth to its social causes, he explained the real

motivation for the social purpose: "If done right, it can inspire consumer loyalty and goodwill . . . but management must 'really believe in it.'"

While KIND uses community in a new way for the snack bar food category, they also produce a premium product. Many competitors make bars from homogeneous pastes, or what some call slab bars. They take whole nuts and fruits and grind them into a paste, adding some stabilizers and artificial ingredients, and creating uniformity. In his book *Do the KIND Thing*, Lubetzky notes that many of his competitors employ these practices because it is more efficient and cost-effective, but he says by doing so they "leave many consumers dissatisfied, as they rob foods of their integrity and soul."

KIND uses whole nuts and fruits, which are more complicated and harder to manufacture than emulsions or paste. KIND Bars fluctuate in size from one bar to the next, and are very often over the package weight, so they don't short the customer. This also sometimes results in bars that are too small; these bars get repurposed for sampling.

The KIND package decision was obvious, but not easy: to showcase the artisan look of whole-nut and fruit bars. It was not an easy package to design. In his book Lubetzky says that he was told, "Real ingredients can't compete with marketers' idealized renditions of food." Slab bars are coated in flavored compounds and sold in foil packaging. Nobody had thought to invest in transparent packaging capable of keeping products fresh. KIND challenged the assumption that nobody wanted to see the bar. The brand has ten values that fall under the "Do the KIND thing" banner, but the tenet that's most critical is "transparency and authenticity." The package delivers on both.

DO YOU KNOW THE SPACE YOU OCCUPY?

CONCLUDING MEMORIES

WHILE BRANDS ARE INTANGIBLE, PHYSICAL PRESENCE IS ESSENTIAL TO DELIVERING MEANING. THERE IS NO FACEBOOK BRAND WITHOUT INTERACTIVE IMAGES ON SCREENS. THIS PRACTICAL VIEW IS ESSENTIAL TO COUNTER THE EXUBERANCE OF A VIRTUAL WORLD. BRANDS ARE INTANGIBLE, BUT RARELY VIRTUAL.

1. We were social beings long before social media, but the invention of these new global mediums gives power to individuals and community with less friction than ever before. This change provides peril and potential for brands.

2. Brands offer economic utility and social utility, amplifying their importance to us in a meritocratic social economy. We use brands to solve problems and to position ourselves in society.

3. Our trust moves along a spectrum from ourselves to our community, and then on to brand handlers to brand owners at the bottom of the trust barrel. Brands need the trust and respect of people, community, and handlers when sending signals.

4. Fame is a matter of scale, and finding influencers within a community is like finding famous people willing to attach their personal brand to your brand. The right signals to the right people can result in a high-velocity brand.

04

BRANDING + SIGNALS

YOU'RE ABOUT TO HEAD DEEPER INTO THE PHYSICAL
DIMENSIONS TO BETTER UNDERSTAND THE ROLE OF
BRAND OWNERS, BRAND HANDLERS, COMMUNITY, AND
PEOPLE. POWER IS SHIFTING WITHIN THESE FOUR
DIMENSIONS AND IT IS FASCINATING TO CONSIDER WHERE
THE CENTER OF GRAVITY IS MOVING FOR BRANDS. IN THE
PAGES AHEAD, WE'LL LOOK AT OLD CONSTRUCTS LIKE
ADVERTISING, PUBLICITY, AND LOYALTY MARKETING AS
SIGNALS FROM THESE FOUR PHYSICAL DIMENSIONS. WE WILL
DECONSTRUCT INTEGRATED MARKETING COMMUNICATIONS
AND EXPLORE WAYS TO REBUILD TRUST AND THE RELATIONSHIP
BETWEEN BRAND OWNERS AND PEOPLE. THE ROLE OF EACH
DISCIPLINE WILL BECOME CLEARER, WITH EXAMPLES OF
SMART ADVERTISING, PUBLICITY, AND LOYALTY MARKETING.
WE SPEAK OF TRUST AND ITS IMPORTANCE TO BRAND
STRENGTH AND FINISH WITH A CASE STUDY OF THE HONEST
COMPANY. SIGNALS LEAD TO EVERYTHING YOU SENSE, FEEL,
AND THINK. SENDING THE RIGHT SIGNALS IS THE CHALLENGE.

EVERYTHING IS SYMBOLIC

BRANDS, BRANDING, AND PEOPLE

Brands don't exist without the voluntary support of customers and the memories they hold, and in many ways, you could say people brand brands. The customer truly is the queen. A brand comes to life through the complex act of branding. What are those branding activities? Everything.

A brand is the result of all intentional and accidental customer experiences. The offering itself is the most potent form of branding, followed by the distribution channels, price, and the marketing communications. In Chapter 3, we explored how people and brands interact in space through networks of communities. This chapter dives deeper into the space dimensions by introducing other players involved in the complex tango between brand owners, signals, and the person experiencing the brand.

Marketing theorist Theodore Levitt said, "People buy products . . . in order to solve problems." The pain of walking great distances was eased by using a horse; the horse was replaced by a car; the car by a plane; the plane by FedEx; and FedEx by Gmail. As the plethora of branded products has exploded, we face an abundance of choice. In meritocratic free market societies, peoples' anxieties about social status is constant, and there is ongoing demand for what economists call positional goods—products that people use to position themselves within social groups.

In addition to the abundance of brand choices, there is also an abundance of media choices. People used to think that having three color TV channels and a remote was a modern wonder. Then we were blown away with the miracle of cable TV. Today YouTube and Google offer millions of channels. Digital distractions are abundant, making it harder for marketers to connect with people. Signals are bombarding us from every direction these days.

Reaching the younger three generations is particularly challenging. Currently defined as generations X, Y, and Z, these three groups start with birthdates from the mid-1960s and

go through present time. They have grown up with mass marketing, advertising, and technology; they have learned from birth the ways and means to filter out branding. The world of branding has seen the signs; long before DVR, there was the TBB (the bathroom break). Human beings have been filtering messages out in a variety of nontechnical ways for decades. It takes energy to think, but less energy to just ignore (filter) these messages. We only have so much cognitive capacity—with the exception, perhaps, for watching cat videos.

Today we are seeing a decline in many of the classic commercial mediums like television, radio, and newsprint. Looking through the models of Space and Time Dimensions we have presented (Chapter 1), we can see a fortress being built by each person, not only filtering out branding from their lives, but also helping others avoid the stink of an intuitively bad customer experience through online reviews and social media comments.

SPACE DIMENSIONS

OF WHAT MEMORIES ARE MADE

Our Space Dimensions model puts the individual person at the center. And nature has designed us to be heavily influenced by family, friends, and trusted colleagues. Today, partially due to the influence of social media, we tend to lump all of these relationships into the category of friends. Whether we can really have 500 friends on Facebook is open to debate. Dunbar's number says our limit is 150 friends. What is certain, however, is that in our fast-changing world, the value of loose connections is increasing. Brands began with relationships with craftspeople. Today we filter brand messages through friends.

Outside this bubble of friends are the entities and human agents that collaborate with the brand owner to carry a message. We call these agents "handlers." Then on the last ring of the model is the brand owner, the makers of the branded offerings, and the orchestrator of all branding efforts. These space dimensions cover

SPACE DIMENSIONS MODEL

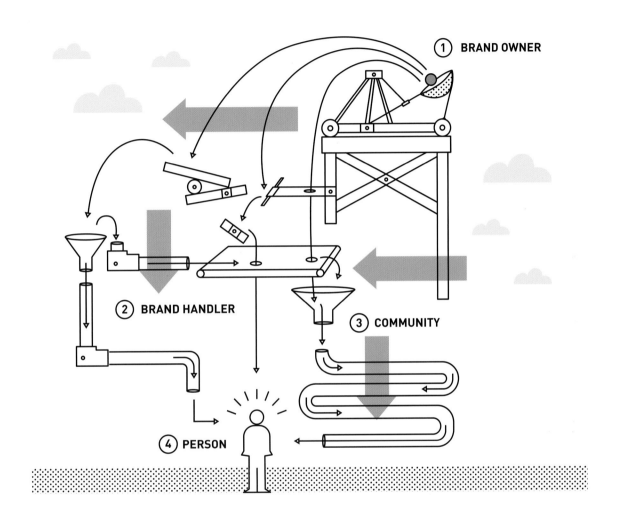

① BRAND OWNER

② BRAND HANDLER

③ COMMUNITY

④ PERSON

WOULD POLLY LIKE AN OLLY?

VITAMINS AND SUPPLEMENTS HAVE ALWAYS BEEN JUST TWO STEPS AWAY FROM MEDICINE, BOTH IN VISUAL LANGUAGE AND TECHNICAL SPEAK. THIS IS COMMON IN CATEGORIES — LEADERS DESIGN CATEGORY PATTERNS AND FOLLOWERS FOLLOW. OLLY WALKED INTO THE CATEGORY AND FLIPPED THIS PILLBOX ON ITS HEAD AND RETHOUGHT THE CATEGORY. OLLY ASKED LEVITT'S QUESTION IN THE SUPPLEMENTS AISLE. PEOPLE DON'T BUY B_{12} AND CALCIUM: THEY BUY ENERGY AND STRONG BONES TO LIVE VIBRANT LIVES. SHOPPING FOR VITAMINS USING B_{12} AS YOUR DECISION-MAKING CRITERIA IS LIKE BUYING AN IPAD FOR THE CIRCUITS. IF YOU DIG A BIT INTO OLLY, YOU'LL SEE THE PHILOSOPHER, ENTREPRENEUR ERIC RYAN FROM METHOD HOME, INVOLVED HERE TOO. SOME MIGHT SAY HE IS PULLING A "METHOD" IN THE VITAMIN AISLE. HIS INNOVATIVE THINKING AND AFFECTION FOR DESIGN GIVES HIM GREATER ODDS OF SUCCESS.

the waterfront of actors in the drama of brands and branding, and through these actors brands are born and die. As you wander through these dimensions—person, community, handler, and owner—consider how your business reality is designed to align.

The person and their friends are insiders; handlers and owners are outsiders. All of these actors operate within immensely complex social systems, filled with multiple feedback systems. Brand owners must navigate barriers to gain the trust of a person. Equations for these four factors translate into models on the effect of branding on brands, as covered in later chapters. Let's start with the brand owner and work our way through layers on the spectrum of trust until we reach the person.

WHOSE ASTERISK IS ON THE LINE?

OWNER OF A BRAND

The brand owner is responsible for protecting and building the brand. The brand owner can be an individual, nonprofit, corporation, retailer, religion, or government organization. Religions and governments were the first major entities to engage in branding on a massive scale. The Great Pyramids of Egypt were not built simply to pass the time, though they certainly took some time to build. Those shining monuments, originally clad with marble, said, "Don't mess with Egypt. Look at how much wealth and slave labor we have." Still not convinced? Consider the brand attributes of the IRS or the CIA. Do they have implied and explicit promises? Imagine someone from the CIA or IRS logo showing up at your door. In some ways, all powerful cultural icons, or memes, are brands.

The challenge for brand owners is to be trusted. We define a brand as a vessel of trust. So while brand owners may enjoy great rewards if a brand becomes desired and valuable, brands are also challenged by a lack of trust in institutions (corporations, government entities, etc.). Brand owners can influence trust through handlers in efforts to influence friends and persons. The fact is, no brand can exist without handlers. The keyword here is influence, as control went bye-bye with the advent of the TV remote and computer mouse.

That said, the brand owner's point of view is obviously essential to the development of a brand. Someone has to give purpose and utility value to a brand and point it in the right direction. Branding is the domain of brand owners and their handlers—their production partners, strategic partners, distributors, sales agents, marketing communication agencies, and consultants. Setting up a business model and brand well in the beginning can mean the difference between a decade of struggle versus rapid acceleration. And once a brand takes off, it requires ongoing vigilance and improvement.

A brand's legal ownership structure influences how a brand is managed and determines a brand's relationship with risk. If a brand is owned by an entrepreneur, things can change on a dime, and risks are easy to take because entrepreneurs tend to love their creations and chase long-term rewards. If a brand is owned by a Delaware corporation (i.e., 499 of the *Fortune* 500), most decisions will be risk averse and focused on short-term gains. Likewise, brands are driven by the corporate culture of the owners, which is an outgrowth of the corporate structure. Brands used to be people, people manage all brands, and all corporations were created by people and are owned by people. Who those people are determines the future of a brand.

Brand leadership is a heavy responsibility depending on the value of the brand in society. Some brands achieve such iconic status that the individual audiences become powerful advocates of the brand and feel the brand is part of their lives. This is all well and fine when leadership is managing the brand to meet customer expectations. Things turn sour when brand managers disappoint customers.

In many ways, you could argue that customers control the brand. Certainly the brand would not exist without customers. A shining example of this is the New Coke story from 1985. Pepsi did empirical research showing that people liked the taste of Pepsi better than Coke, and they advertised this fact throughout the Pepsi Challenge. In response, Coke changed their formula and taste profile, and in response, Coke fans got angry. Really angry! This story ended well for Coke because sales actually rose after they returned to the original taste. But it could have become a disaster if the owners of the Coke brand did not listen to customers.

TO BUILD A BRAND, IT STARTS WITH A HANDLER

HANDLERS OF BRANDS

Brand building is a team sport, and brand owners and their teams serve as captains. All handlers are part of the brand. Dozens, sometimes thousands, of entities may be involved in the production of the product or service. Oat farmers are part of the Cheerios brand, for example, and so are third-party millers, manufacturers, suppliers, distributors, retailers, dealers, resellers, agencies, consultants, mass media, and social media. Everyone in the value chain has to do his or her part to make a great brand. Though not without controversy, Apple and Nike have mastered this art, both in the supply chain and in brand communications. And Walmart has become so expert at managing factories in Asia and around the globe that it measurably improved productivity numbers in the United States.

Once upon a time, integrated marketing communications was the ultimate dream: Giant media conglomerates would be able to use computers to orchestrate and control all the messages "consumers" received, leading to robotic purchasing behavior. The Internet obliterated that dream. Nevertheless, brand owners do need to put their message out there in a fractured and treacherous media landscape, and they do so through the product itself, events, public relations, advertising, their Internet footprint, and social media. Outside handlers from communication agencies are typically involved in all of these activities.

There are two recent developments making it more challenging for brand owners to handle the handlers. The first change is the unbundling of production and distribution. In a world of rising complexity, few vertically integrated firms remain. Multiple aspects of a business are outsourced, the supply chain is integrated, sales channel conflicts are navigated, and communication agents are managed.

The second major development is the changing media landscape. Mass media is in decline, and using history as a guide, it will likely continue to slowly drop and then suddenly fall. The reach and frequency models that powered brand advertising are already broken. The prime actor in this drama is the Internet. The Internet is probably equal to the impact of the printing press multiplied by ten. Some call the current generation the YouTube generation, as they have little interest outside of their phones and tablets. And boomers are struggling to keep up.

This is not to say that the current media companies will entirely go away. Instead, they will likely migrate to the Internet as shadows of their former selves. Media entities are brands themselves as well as handlers for other brands, and one of the most interesting dramas is the titanic battle between CNN and FOX News.

When we say separate "brand owner" and include media, you might think we consider CNN and Fox News to be brands. Yes, we do, and you should, too. The truth is hard to hear, but both are brands and are managed as such. Brands need trust to survive and media certainly needs to be a trusted source for information. As an example, the mere existence of FOX News is one of the least talked about yet most compelling brand stories in the past few decades. Put aside all the political rhetoric and consider these two as brands.

FOX News took almost half the market in much less than a decade by building a brand around a belief system and an audience willing to listen. If you believe CNN was delivering the truth and FOX News was spewing lies, then you're still shrouded in your personal political belief system. Both sources put out their "version" of the truth and you have the joy of figuring out who's telling the story with more accuracy. To take it down another layer, both of these "commercial" news channels exist to serve up emotionally engaged audiences to advertisers.

The next big handlers are in the manufacturing and supply chain, then on to outside sales reps and retailers. Retailers, while also brand owners themselves, have a closer relationship with their shoppers than the brands they carry. Retailers know who's buying what, when, and where.

Let's use Target as a great example of a high-fashion, low-cost retailer. When Target shelves a brand, they don't just buy it and push it through a distribution system to give people a way to buy it: They endorse the brand. People are more likely to trust something they find on the shelves at Target versus down the street at a garage sale. Nothing against your neighbor's annual garage sale, but we're not buying our coffee beans there.

Being on the shelf at Target has meaning and value beyond what shows up in the transaction. Sure, Target makes it easy to buy something versus sourcing it from a Chinese factory yourself. But that isn't the greatest value this particular handler offers. When Target is successful, they have offered all the items you need and some you didn't know you needed but couldn't find anywhere else. This means a successful retailer is a curator of offerings and provider of an experience, carefully selecting the brands they endorse.

Handlers such as retailers offer some level of objectivity and therefore can move up a few steps on the trust spectrum. These third-party handlers include the news media and distribution, and the story even becomes more interesting when you consider partner brands, industry experts, nonprofits, and suppliers. All of these handlers are elements in a complex system. Yes, it's easy to get lost amid the trees in this forest.

So let's open this menagerie to include all other potential third parties and discuss some interesting heat sources. In the history of Jelly Belly, their defining moment was most likely the time a California governor, Ronald Reagan, quit smoking and took to eating Jelly Belly jelly beans as a substitute. His rise to president of the United States certainly didn't hurt the brand's awareness and cultural relevance. When Reagan used bags of Jelly Belly to court congressional Democrats, the Jelly Belly brand was catapulted into popular culture. Our modern version of this would be the revitalization of Gap when Michelle Obama gave them her comfortable nod of appreciation.

The second law of thermodynamics, also known as entropy, is always at play. A large heat source at one moment in time can suck all the oxygen out of a room if it is not replenished. Consider the staged endorsements made by athletes, movie stars, and cultural celebrities. For example, Lady Gaga made a special trip to the Consumer Electronics Show (CES) in Las Vegas to endorse Polaroid in 2011. Have you heard anything else since? How relevant is Polaroid today? This is a classic example of a large heat source offering a brand endorsement and then the energy dissipating not long after.

Now consider those situations when the endorsers are not superstars but mom bloggers with thousands of followers each. Collectively these blogs attract millions of readers. The gathering of many smaller versions of such endorsements has less risk and more impact for a brand's energy level. Building a base of thousands of mom bloggers to endorse and rave about your baby products over the course of a year will have a more sustainable impact. The multiple sources of heat spark other sources of heat as these moderately influential bloggers touch other bloggers and social influencers. This is the scale-free network in action. The outcome is a more sustainable approach to building brand energy than a sparkling fashionista with glamorous wearable meat giving your brand a nod.

And then we have causes, nonprofits, and organizations, all doing well while doing good. There are a number of reasons brands with baked-in higher purpose are generally doing well: They have the ability to counter the lowered trust. Toms Shoes can be trusted because they are giving one pair of shoes away to someone in need for every pair you buy. Emotion is the most powerful human energy source.

Building a brand without third-party endorsements is possible, but not recommended. It just makes the hill that much steeper and the rock heavier. Ask Mark Twain's Tom Sawyer about whitewashing a fence: It's always more fun if you can get your friends to help.

ADVICE FROM YOUR COMMUNITY

The fundamental question to determine loyalty for brands is to ask someone if she would refer the brand to family or friends. Simple. Why does this work? People are likely to trust other people more than an organization. Most likely you'll have to face that person someday, and if you've put your name behind a brand, you make it part of your story. And we don't like to walk around with egg on our face.

Online communities have gained exponential influence and power over the past decade. This is similar to the growth of brand handlers, specifically retailers, in the past two decades. Before the Internet, if you were considering making a purchase of a titanium bicycle branded Moots, you'd check with your friends. It's a big purchase; typically a Moots sells for $3,500 just for the frame—not even a seat is included. The process to check with your friends included calls, perhaps letters, and in-person conversations. Now you can do it all online.

Today, the ability for a brand to transfer heat from one person to another is much more efficient. Likewise, the opportunity for haters to apply heat to a brand is much more efficient. Now we can see what the brands' friends surround themselves with during an adventure. Without meaning to, we are receiving implied endorsements from our friends based on what they're wearing or where they traveled on spring break.

The growth of social media as a method to gather more energy from friends, colleagues, and family can be correlated to the falling trust in institutions. When people lose trust in institutions, they clamor for more transparency. Friends, family, and colleagues—our community—fills the vacuum. We seek sources to trust and meaning in our lives just as plants seek sunlight. Our community transmits both positive and negative energy for brands today, second only to what we draw from our own experience.

If you're a brand owner, you've probably asked the question, "How do we get to the communities?" Over time, the answers have moved from traveling peddlers, to main-street merchants, to telemarketers, to big-box retailers, to online merchants, to spam e-mail, to pay-per-click ads, and social media. It starts to crumble around the edges when the salesperson or retailer starts to act like a selfish robot in an organization. Selling something for the sake of making a sale is a shallow relationship. And friends don't let friends sell for multilevel marketing.

So how else do you get to people through communities? Product placement is another covert marketing method. Get a notable celebrity to handle your brand, use it, and get photographed by the paparazzi—preferably on a nearly nude beach she thought was private. While notable individuals can offer a huge influx of heat for a brand, they act more like handlers than community, so the apertures of trust contract quickly. Once you are a celebrity handler, you're acting like a corporation, not a trusted advisor. Getting your brand in their hands has more integrity if it happens because they believe in your brand. Paying to be in a grab bag of freebies at the Oscars will only get you so far.

As a brand owner, what is the best way to reach larger communities? Taking one moment at a time with deliberate consideration for why they would have a relationship with your brand. That's how we build trust with friends, and that's how brands build trust with a person.

YOUR EXPERIENCE, YOUR CHOICE

ONE PERSON

All your friends have tried the new "new" thing, and you've seen how happy they are in their Instagram photos. You've seen a few ads on TV, driven past billboards, and you've even read online reviews. You are starting to get the itch. Last night you saw your object of desire on the news and the anchor seemed so excited he could hardly contain himself. You see yourself as an independent thinker and you treasure your freedom and autonomy, but you are starting to feel like the last person who hasn't taken the leap. You are your own last line of defense. So you visit the store, touch it, try it, and talk to a noncommissioned,

cotton-candy friendly employee. You pick out the perfect color and take a moment to see how it looks in your hand. This is the moment of decision, so you want to make sure you get it right. Your social reputation is on the line.

The smiling, uniformed staffer comes over again and asks you if that's the one you'd like. She disappears for a few minutes, comes back smiling with your box, hands it to you. You slowly open the top feeling the precious nature of this moment. There it is, shining back at you with a beautiful sparkle from the store's lighting. You pluck it from its precise cradle, hold it in your hand between your fingers, and look at it for just a moment. You can feel the substance. You can feel the thoughtfulness of whoever took the time to design this precious beauty. The banter from your friends about taking the leap is now falling away as you see yourself in the black mirror. The chemical oxytocin is pumping. You are falling in love.

Welcome to the latest iPhone from Apple.

This is one of the most compelling moments designed for anyone willing and barely able to drop $600 to $800 on this precious jewel of technology. It is a designed moment for a luxury electronics brand. Designed for you and millions like you. If you found comparisons to buying jewelry, that's certainly deliberate. If you found yourself salivating and twitching for a trip to the local Apple Store, that's also deliberate. We see ourselves as rational actors in an irrational world, but the truth is, we buy on emotion and justify with facts.

LET IN SOME LIGHT, SEE WHAT GROWS

THE APERTURE OF TRUST

Let's go to an example in the real world today, Uber. There are two large camps forming around this highly successful venture. The first, people who have tried an Uber ride, enjoyed it so much they will suffer when trying to go back to a traditional cab. The other camp is concerned about safety, and has heard scary stories about

THOUGHT EXPERIMENT

WHAT IS THE APPLE LOYALTY PROGRAM?

Uber drivers or consumed signals about the risks of this new type of ride.

The first excuse for not trying Uber is usually, "I don't feel comfortable getting into a car with a stranger." Then, if you asked, isn't a cab defined as a car with a stranger, the answer is, "Yes, but what keeps the Uber driver from kidnapping you?" And, when you respond with the logical statement, "What keeps the cabbie from doing the same?" you distill it down to the fact that a cab has a registration number on the side. Yet the Uber system records your connection to the person who picked you up. Negative signals keep many people from trusting an Uber; no matter whether they receive seven or seventeen signals, their aperture of trust is not allowing much light in at all. Habits are hard to change until the masses are all running in the same direction, perhaps with yellow cabs chasing them.

As we age and gain life experiences, our aperture of trust tends to close down to brand owners and brand handlers. You can see this as a general loss of optimism, but in actuality it is a human interest and a move toward realism. Although brand owners can gain trust over time and cause our apertures to their signals to dilate, if owners make promises, implied and explicit, and then break those promises, we once again contract our apertures to their signals.

A BIG BOX DESIGNED BY BIG THINKERS

THE CULT OF COSTCO

Costco is an amazing container of trust. The name and graphic identity seem generic. The buildings are utilitarian warehouses with cement floors, cinder-block walls, and klieg lights. So why is Costco consistently voted a top retailer by Consumer Reports? The answer is in how they have designed the business. Costco curbs customer anxiety by limiting choice, thereby increasing buying power. Then they mark up prices at one rate across the board to cover expenses. All of Costco's $2 billion annual profit comes from annual member fees. The way Costco makes a profit focuses everyone on the customer experience, even the buyers. Costco designed the business to be focused on you and your experience. When customers become friends, you don't have to pay many brand handlers. Costco's members are their best ads.

BRANDING ISN'T ADVERTISING, ADVERTISING IS BIG IN BRANDING

IMPACT ON ADVERTISING

If we believed everything we heard in advertising and had no other sources of input (media, friends, product use, etc.), then advertising would be branding. But since we are not robots and actually have friends, colleagues, feelings, and existing belief systems, branding is not advertising. Though, advertising is an important part of branding as it defines the brand's worldview. It is the message directly from the corporation; therefore, it clarifies how they see the world and what they want you to hear. We take these messages with a large grain of salt. But how we interpret these messages is more important than our lack of trust.

Mass production, massive transportation and distribution systems, mass communications, and mass advertising drove the industrial revolution. It all led to standardized products at a lower cost and better prices. As brands have moved to fill niches and as communication systems have become fragmented by cable TV and now the Internet, the charm and effectiveness of mass advertising has fallen. The Mad Men marked the end of an era. Today advertising is a high-risk game.

Some still try to use advertising the old way. Here's the essence of an arcane way of thinking: If we "hit" customers enough times (nine or more is the most recent standard; once it was three hits) with this message, they will be aware of our product and buy it.

"Hit" me once with your message, shame on you; "hit" me twice, shame on me for not ducking or pressing FFWD on my DVR remote. This may be part of the reason advertising as a word and philosophy has fallen so far out of favor. If this is news to you, consider that the Cannes Lions International Festival of Advertising awards has recently replaced "Advertising" with "Creativity" in its title.

Advertising is still a good way to spark word of mouth when you actually have something new to say or something innovative to offer. But during the 1970s, the ad media buyers' logic was that if you interrupted programming enough times, people could not help but notice and buy your brand. The blowback from decades of media saturation has resulted in a jaded and suspicious public, and the decline in commercial-supported media has made the environment worse. Much of current mass-media advertising is defensive in nature, trying to thwart competition and convince people that tired products are still cool. Yet the original "1984" TV spot for the Macintosh computer ran a grand total of one time. There are other routes to fame and fortune.

Advertising controls messages and then an external or internal handler filters and spins them into something interesting. Ads express the brand owner's point of view, with little room for engagement or interaction. Over the last fifty years advertising has been exploited to drive sales, put awards on the walls of agencies, and serve the short-term needs of brand managers.

BUYING LOYALTY IS A LIABILITY

LOYALTY MARKETING

Can you name an airline you'd refer to as a neighborhood friend whom you like and respect? Few are likely to come to mind—perhaps Cathay Pacific, Virgin, JetBlue, or Singapore Airlines. Most U.S. travelers struggle with their relationships with airline brands. And for that matter, the airlines struggle with their relationship with customers as well. The skies have not been very friendly over the past two decades.

Fluctuating fuel prices, overbooking passengers to fill every seat, and the disintermediation of travel agents has challenged the relationship between an airline and its passengers. Add the invention of loyalty programs designed to exchange points for loyalty in situations where loyalty isn't required (the hub-and-spoke system of air travel limits options), and you have a recipe for trouble. These points are now the currency that customers want to exchange for the promise of future flights. But airlines control the value and accessibility of the currency. So this paid-for loyalty becomes a customer complaint and an airline liability on the balance sheet. Yet this type of thinking is still rampant in the world of loyalty marketing.

While buying loyalty is a liability, earning it is not. It all comes down to the right context.

WHAT DOES REFRESHING FEEL LIKE?

THE DESIGN OF THE COCA-COLA BOTTLE WAS INTENDED TO BE DISTINCT ENOUGH TO ALLOW SOMEONE TO IDENTIFY HIS OR HER CHOICE OF COLA IN THE DARK. THE BOTTLE DESIGNER HAD TO FOCUS ON ONE SENSE FIRST IN ORDER TO ENSURE THE DESIGN COULD BE DISTINCT WITHOUT THE NAME COCA-COLA. THE SHAPE OF THE BOTTLE, RIDGES, AND WEIGHT ALL CONTRIBUTED TO A UNIQUE FEEL THAT COULD BE OWNED BY COCA-COLA. WHILE THE IDEA OF GRABBING YOUR NEXT COKE BOTTLE IN PITCH BLACK DOESN'T SEEM TOO LIKELY, THE RESULT IS A DISTINCT BOTTLE THAT QUICKLY BECAME ICONIC. IT'S EASY TO FORGET THE IMPORTANCE OF SOME OF OUR SENSES. BUT DESIGNED MOMENTS CAN BE AS PRECISE AS A BOTTLE SHAPE.

An individual may not claim to be loyal to one brand but exhibit loyal behaviors when facing the moment of decision. Then loyalty becomes an unspoken feeling: "I am always loyal to Coca-Cola, because Coke is my brand."

People are loyal to moments if they are properly designed. An internal voice may say, "I always go to Target grocery on Tuesday mornings because it isn't crazy busy and for some reason I find the best deals on Tuesday." This focus on moments of truth allows brand owners to focus marketing resources to deliver meaningful experiences that earn customer loyalty.

TELL THE TRUTH BUT MANAGE THE MESSAGE

PUBLIC RELATIONS AND PUBLICITY

They say advertising is what you pay for and PR is what you pray for. Publicity builds awareness and helps manage the reputation of the brand owner. Unless you've been locked in a cubicle for the past decade, storytelling has seen exponential growth when it comes to methods of building brand value.

Many brands are built on the efforts of public relations and publicity with little or no mass advertising. To list a few you might know, Patagonia, the Honest Company, GoPro, KIND Bars, and Costco. These brands also provide us with great examples of how great business models, storytelling, and an internally consistent narrative can contribute to a brand's momentum. Patagonia has embedded storytelling into their culture. Every effort, no matter if it will be seen by customers or not, has a narrative thread inside Patagonia. The Honest Company has blended celebrity influence and responsible products for the modern family to build a brand using the conversations between loving and highly social moms. And GoPro has built a platform to share the adventures of their customers' highly dramatic stunts in hi-definition video. They essentially built a brand around sharing evidence of life's greatest adventures and tallest tales.

This discipline of public relations has made

THE ORIGINAL RESPONSIBLE BRAND

YVON CHOUINARD DESIGNED PATAGONIA AS A RESPONSIBLE BRAND LONG BEFORE SUSTAINABILITY WAS A BUZZWORD AND GREEN WAS THE COLOR OF CHOICE FOR BRANDS ATTEMPTING TO CLEAN UP THEIR RELATIONSHIP WITH THE PLANET. THE STORYTELLING HERITAGE OF THE BRAND CONTINUES TODAY AND HAS ALLOWED THE BRAND TO REMAIN RELEVANT, RESPECTED, AND RESPONSIBLE IN A MODERN, CONSUMPTION-DRIVEN ECONOMY. AS AN INDICATION OF HOW STORY-DRIVEN THIS BRAND IS, THEIR SELECTION CRITERIA FOR A NEW PARTNER TO REDESIGN THEIR BASE-LAYER PACKAGING INCLUDES THE QUESTION, "WOULD YOU SPEND A WEEK IN A TENT WITH THESE PEOPLE?" TRUST IN THE PEOPLE BEHIND THE BRAND IS BAKED RIGHT INTO THE CULTURE AND BECOMES A BINDING THREAD IN ALL THAT THEY DO TO OFFER RESPONSIBLY DESIGNED, MANUFACTURED, AND DELIVERED PRODUCTS TO THE PLANET. A BRAND DESIGNED FOR PEOPLE AND THE PLANET.

huge strides from the early 1900s when the Rockefeller family repaired their reputation after the Ludlow Massacre. These early practices of "damage control" go by the current name "crisis communications." While this remains some of the highest-billing work for PR agents, it isn't known to inspire a human soul. As brands get pulled into or walk themselves into situations where public opinion is not in their favor, enter the crisis communicator. They bill at a price similar to the lawyer who gets you out of jail on the night before your wedding.

This is where you ask the question, "Isn't 'any publicity, good publicity' a common belief?" Well, that phrase has a bit lopped off the end of it. "If you have nothing else going on at all," then yes, talking about you negatively is at least something. This publicity, though negative, is still energy. Look at it this way: If brand energy is the wind, negative publicity is wind blowing against your sails and the lack of wind altogether is a complete lack of publicity. So if the wind is working against you, adjust your sails.

MARTHA KNOWS THE RIGHT RECIPE

MODEL ON PRISON TIME

One of the best examples of adjusting your sails to turn negative energy into positive energy is Martha Stewart. She spent time in prison for SEC violations and took on her term with positive, creative spirit. Rumors leaked of her teaching cooking and decorating classes on the inside (giving back to her fellow inmates). After serving her sentence, she spoke frankly about her regret and the challenge of spending time behind bars. This premium brand known for beautiful details designed into everything was "a good thing" until the ink dried on a brand distribution deal with Kmart.

The manner in which Martha Stewart managed her prison time arguably contributed to her brand value in the end, although we wouldn't recommend it to anyone. On the other hand, the deal with Kmart probably destroyed value.

While the distribution deal certainly delivered revenue for the Martha brand, and Kmart received more traffic, the warm glow of the Martha brand was dimmed by the additional revenue. Kmart as a retailer creates a disconnect with Martha's typical brand fanatic. There were certainly plenty of Martha followers who responded to the Kmart deal with the question, "Really, Martha Stewart will be exclusively at Kmart?"

DISINTEGRATED MARKETING COMMUNICATIONS

UNBUNDLING THE MARKETING MIX

Looking at our four factors of Space (brand owner, handler, community, person) and considering the current and near-future state of affairs, what would you do? The average person's trust aperture is so nearly closed off to the brand owners, it is a wonder any light gets through. Brand owners, and for that matter educational institutions, have been rearranging the pieces of integrated mass-media marketing communications plans so many ways, there seem to be few untested scenarios left. We ask the question, should marketing be disintegrated? Or is the discipline of marketing too large and facing a dinosaur death?

In the 1980s and 1990s power shifted in favor of mass retailers, and with the growth of Amazon and consolidation in media conglomerates this is a permanent state for now. And the 2000s and 2010s have seen the power of community as social media and recommendations have become immensely accessible and prolific. Brand owners often find their direct signals to the person are blocked or met with skepticism, distrust, and sometimes even anger. Instead, brand owners try to deliver signals through handlers and community, ceding control in exchange for effectiveness.

We don't believe marketing is facing death, but the body of knowledge is certainly on life support. We have "thought leaders" and pontificators giving out bits and pieces, but it hasn't all come together with a clear view of the future. What we do know is if we're going to make progress a few things need to be addressed:

We need a renewed empathy for the human being, not as consumer, audience, or segment, but as a person.

We need to unbundle and re-evaluate all pieces of integrated marketing communications and see which ones are working and for what purpose.

We need a unifying theory or philosophy between the customer experience and the brand-marketing schools of thinking.

BE THE NODE, NOT THE KNOB

THE HONEST COMPANY

Ever have a moment when you see someone in person who looks really familiar, like you've had him over for dinner or met him for coffee, but you just can't place how you know him? Then you realize he is a local celebrity or news personality. We invite other people into our lives through media channels. We interact with them daily, weekly, or hourly perhaps. They achieve a status of awareness in our memories and credibility if they've managed their reputation properly. Then they start to leverage their name for their fiscal benefit and that of other brands they endorse. It might be as minimal as pitching a product in a commercial or as elaborate as having their own fashion line, shoes, or perfume. This transition from a person you consider having celebrity status to a celebrity brand is a dangerous one. Now, as a brand handler, people are less likely to trust the person behind the celebrity façade.

Yet we see a company built with a celebrity inside is a new perspective. The Honest Company is a brand with a celebrity founder, not a celebrity brand. The distinction is important and goes to the purpose behind the brand. The purpose of a celebrity brand is to parse out a bit of the celebrities' lifestyle in the form of fashion they wear, perfume they use, or the shoes they prance around in sometimes. The purpose of The Honest Company is this: "Everything that touches you and your family—everything in your home—needs to be nontoxic, needs to be effective and beautiful to look at, and needs to be affordable," says Jessica Alba. This defines a celebrity on a mission, starting a brand with two other partners versus a celebrity brand.

Now let's start with the exponential growth curve in a stagnant, brand-heavyweight category like diapers. Don't we have a fair amount of respectable, smart, seasoned marketing minds at the other *Fortune* 500 companies selling diapers to moms? What advantage does Ms. Alba and her team have over these big boys with big budgets?

What about the relationship between a mom and her child? There exists no stronger human bond. So consider the brands previously in this relationship—name your favorite diaper brand— and get a bit curious about the chemicals used in the product and manufacturing process. Whether these chemicals are harmful or not, they are labeled chemicals.

What about these old vessels of trust— existing brands in the diaper category—with history, heritage, and plenty of dollars to spend on advertising and promotions. Perhaps they have been innovating in the wrong areas? What is the most important moment when purchasing a diaper, if you don't have previous experience?

At the retail shelf when mom is reading the package and discovering a better design, more responsible ingredients, and an intentional avoidance of "perceived to be" harmful chemicals. This is where The Honest Company has their first advantage, ironically at the P&G "moment of truth" when Pampers has to face the truth.

Have you heard of a responsible disposable diaper? If you don't have hippie parents and the cloth diaper pin scars in your hips, it might sound like an oxymoron. What diaper brand would innovate toward a more responsible and expensive diaper when the benefits are not yet clear? The answer inside might sound like this: "No one else in the category is selling a more responsible diaper." What brand would innovate in this direction? Certainly not a corporation looking to retain share in a historic brand.

An upstart doesn't have to worry about market share leaking out, because all market share is upward growth. And who better to out-innovate the old boys than a mom (Jessica Alba) protecting her children from "the big, bad corporation." The Honest Company has the ideal built-in social spokesperson, plenty of stories to share in social, and a product to match the potential scale of a modern brand-heroic story.

REMEMBER THE VEGAS TATTOO? BEGRUDGINGLY, YES

CONCLUDING MEMORIES

THIS CHAPTER SHOULD HAVE LEFT SOME PHYSICAL IMPRESSIONS IN YOUR MEMORY. HERE ARE A FEW THOUGHTS WE INTENDED TO LEAVE YOU WITH, AND IF THAT DIDN'T OCCUR, THESE CONCLUSIONS WILL MAKE THE POINT.

(1) Branding is everything. With the amount of choices and signals sent to us, branding is both essential and hard to control. A brand is the result of all signals, leading to moments and memories.

(2) Brand owners are outsiders and furthest away from the community and person, which results in trust issues. It's important for brand owners to have direct experience with the people and communities they serve.

(3) Handlers are also outsiders, but often closer to the person, and necessary for branding. Since handlers are an extension of the brand, it is important to manage them with both caution and respect.

(4) A community contributes to the brand as the first level of insiders: people. It is easy to trust a friend and important for people to be accepted by a community, which makes the community an essential part of individual decisions.

(5) A person's experience with a brand is the ultimate form of branding, as a person's first moment can change everything she thinks she knows about a brand. When that word spreads within a community, brand energy spreads with velocity.

(6) Branding may include advertising, loyalty programs, and publicity. But these aspects alone are not branding. How branding activities and systems are mixed and managed define the effectiveness and influence of the brand.

05

SIGNALS + SENSES

IN THIS CHAPTER, TAKE A SWIM IN THE WARM WAVES OF
THE FIVE PRIMARY SENSES: SIGHT, SOUND, TOUCH, TASTE,
AND SMELL. REAL SURFING HAS SALT, SAND, AND THE RISK
OF YOUR SURFBOARD BEING BROKEN IN HALF BY A MON-
STER WAVE. OUR EXPLORATION IS LESS RISKY. WE'LL SURF
IDEAS ON THE IMPORTANCE OF MEMORIES AND HOW THE SIG-
NALS ARE USED BY OUR SENSES TO MAKE MEMORIES. YOU'LL
MEET THE ORIGINAL NEUROSCIENTIST, EXPLORE CLAM-
SHELL PACKAGES, AND RECONSIDER HOW YOU TASTE THE
SUPERFOOD (AND NOT SO SUPER YUMMY) KALE. YOU'LL TAKE
A NEW LOOK AT THE CONCEPT OF BEAUTY THROUGH THE
LENS OF MATHEMATICS, SEE LOGOS THROUGH THE EYES OF
RATS, AND GET UP CLOSE AND PERSONAL WITH YOU AND THE
LARGEST ORGAN—YOUR SKIN. QUEUE THE BEACH BOYS. SIT
BACK AND ENJOY THE RIDE.

WE CONSUME IN WAVES

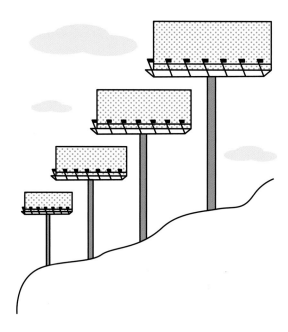

To become famous, a brand must find a home as a memory planted in and retrieved from billions of neurons. Each person has multiple barriers between themselves and signals from brands. In Chapter 4, we discussed the barriers of closed apertures of trust to signals from brand owners and the fragmented media used to send signals. There are also barriers from the noisy clutter of messages and distractions that mask the signals. In our always-on, hyper-connected world, attention is the scarcest human resource.

Sensory signals clamor for attention every waking instant. But, before we get too far into the five senses you know (sight, sound, smell, taste, and touch), let's acknowledge the other senses not commonly discussed like balance, acceleration, temperature, kinesthetic, pain, and even the sense of time. While these are essential for our humanity, for this effort we have chosen to consider them for future study.

So neuroscientists have figured out that our brains do a lot of editing. Photons bounce off objects, enter our eyes, and one in a million

signals reach awareness. Legions of other signals are also cut from what we touch, hear, taste, and smell. All the signals remaining combine with memory and our current emotional state to inform ideas and actions, leading to yet more sensory data, and on it goes.

A big change for marketers is that the Internet has given people more power for discernment than ever before. Carve out a moment—ninety seconds—from your trip to work. Driving down the freeway to work, you consume five billboards. The billboards are sending signals and you are consuming these signals, but in many cases, if asked when you get to work what billboards you saw or even how many, you'd have to guess. The 100 percent post-consumer-waste paper cup you hold sends signals of quality coffee or your thin-walled polystyrene foam cup sends signals of an unfortunate gas station choice.

The taste of your coffee as you careen down the freeway sends signals of the caffeine choices you've made in life, from the single pour at a local coffee shop to a quality cup of Starbucks joe. And perhaps there is the faint smell of greasy potatoes as you spot some of your kids' discarded french fries moldering on the car mat. The distinct sound of a Harley-Davidson motorcycle pulls up next to you and you can feel the engine vibration through your door. And this is a mere ninety seconds or less of an eighteen-hour, or 64,800-second, day we spend consuming signals. You would think with all the capacity of our brains and the number of seconds in a day, brands would have a better chance of having a signal reach long-term memory. But brands are dealing with brains that process signals like monkeys swinging from tree to tree. Consciousness is a highly random and inscrutable process.

While our signal-consuming brain is a gluttonous blue-ribbon pig, our long-term memory is a superficial supermodel with a photo shoot in the morning. Your senses consume these signals as waves or vibrations and your brain turns them into data to be processed. A small sampling of these signals hit the processing areas of your brain, but the vast majority get lost in your subconscious. Your brain does not consume any of these signals in a vacuum nor does it make a judgment until the signals are processed through cognitive centers of the brain. Your brain consumes signals all day long. Signals are the smallest measurable contribution we will explore. The right waves of signals can lead to a designed moment.

MOMENTS THAT MATTER

BRANDS LIVE IN MEMORY

We know that experiences stimulate neural activity, and actions such as purchasing or using a product are the result of neural activity. Together, these actions turn into memories, giving life to brands. Immersive multisensory experiences over time are more likely to create memorable moments, and increasing involvement over time strengthens these memories to grow consistent habits and strong brands. People and brand interactions across time and space are an indication of what is going on inside of brains. Direct measurement of the full extent of this neural activity is a different, difficult, and future matter, but more is known today about what's going on upstairs than ever before. And it's clear that experience with the brand offering is central.

THE ORIGINAL NEUROSCIENTIST?

ABOUT 2,500 YEARS AGO, SITTING BENEATH THE BODHI TREE, SIDDHARTHA GAUTAMA CAME UP WITH INSIGHTS THAT NEUROSCIENTISTS ARE STILL STUDYING TODAY. ONE OF HIS INSIGHTS WAS THAT CONSCIOUSNESS HAS FIVE AGGREGATES: MATTER, FEELING, THINKING, IMPULSES, DISCERNMENT. TODAY NEUROSCIENTISTS ARE STUDYING THE BRAINS OF BUDDHIST MONKS, AND MONKS ARE STUDYING THE RESEARCH OF NEUROSCIENTISTS. EVEN THE DALAI LAMA IS PART OF THIS QUEST. BOTH MONKS AND NEUROSCIENTISTS HAVE DISCOVERED THE PRIMACY OF EMOTION. THE WESTERN ENLIGHTENMENT SOUGHT TO MAKE REASON KING, BUT WE NOW KNOW THAT FEELINGS COME FIRST.

THOUGHT EXPERIMENT

HOW LONG WOULD IT TAKE TO COUNT THE SIGNALS BRANDS ARE SENDING YOU IN ONE EIGHTEEN-HOUR DAY?

The full workings of a brain are still a great riddle. Some proclaim it is a riddle as large as the workings of the universe. Physicists are using telescopes to search for a grand unified theory of the universe, and neuroscientists are using brain scans and other new tools to search for a unified theory of the brain. In both instances, we are far from comprehensive answers, and many believe we'll never solve all the mysteries. There are about 100 billion galaxies in the observable universe and 86 billion neurons in a human brain. We call 94 percent of the universe dark matter or dark energy, because we know it exists but don't know what it is. The consciousness you are currently experiencing is an utter mystery. We are in way over our heads.

So enjoy the little nuggets of what we do know about the relationship between memory and experiences as they relate to brands and branding. Consider the following cerebral popcorn to point us in the right direction.

MEMORIES BORN OF EXPERIENCE

DESIGNED FOR WHOM?

Having an experience requires sensory input. We receive sensory input from inside the womb, so you've been enjoying experiences since Mom was rubbing you through her belly. Though you're likely unable to explicitly remember any of your experiences before turning four years old, you may be able to access an implicit memory of an object or a scent. So during those early years you contributed to other's experiences, and in doing so, you made explicit memories for your parents, grandparents, and even your annoying big sister. But before we go further into memory we need to define an experience.

What exactly is an experience anyway? The philosophical answer is that an experience is the accumulation over time of thoughts and feelings gathered by perception, consumed through our senses, and then remembered. Significant aspects of an experience are time, input from senses, and the ability to remember.

Experiences can be parceled out into moments or explicitly memorable experiences. But since time can speed up and slow down, having specificity in seconds is really not as important as the thoughts and emotions in a moment itself. And the emotions an experience creates loom large.

Consider your recent negative or positive experiences and ponder how they could be redesigned. If you can deconstruct experiences, you can dig deeper and design moments that contribute to positive memories across time and space. From here you might be thinking, how many experiences are actually intentionally designed? As a whole, not many. Either the experience wasn't given much thought at all or it was designed by the designer for the designer. To succeed, designed experiences need to move from me to they to we.

Clamshell packages for electronics protect high-value items sold in retail and are a great example of a bad experience. Who was at the center of that designed moment? Unless you're Mr. Edward Scissorhands, it wasn't designed for you. Though there was a person at the center of this designed experience, that person was a thief, not a customer. Clamshells are designed for thieves!

Greater knowledge of these moments can lead to positive and negative rankings, like things that matter and those that anti-matter. Pardon the cheesy mixed metaphors, but we couldn't help ourselves. In the clamshell example, a moment was designed to negatively impact the thief, you, and the planet. Yet it was designed to positively impact the brand owner and handler (manufacturer and retailer). To this day, the utility value of what's inside offers enough motivation to carve into these packages: It's been great for scissor sales.

Moments make a contribution to brand utility when they embed positive long-term memories, which, let's be honest, is not an easy task with this gray matter we have bobbing around on top of our spine. So how do we make the moment matter? (Hint: the answer is all around you.)

THE ULTIMATE CONNOISSEURS?

SENSORY INPUTS TO MEMORY

Was Superman a supertaster, too? Connoisseurs are admired for their ability to raise consumption to a noble art. It can take decades of living large to fully appreciate a $1,000 bottle of wine. But most professional tasters, known as supertasters, take it to a genetically enhanced level because they have a specific gene, found in 25 percent of the world population. It is associated with tongues with more of a certain type of taste bud and the ability to taste a strong bitterness in certain foods. That's not to say they enjoy the taste. They just have a super ability to discern the taste. Along with the supertasters' extra dose of taste buds, they have larger areas of their gray matter devoted to processing taste signals.

Your brain and the brain of your college roommate, Jack, do not have the same sensory wiring. For example, an estimated 1 in 2,000 people have synesthesia, a condition in which more than one sensory processing path may process the same sensory information, such as "seeing" a color when a pitch is heard or an emotion is felt. Designers, as a collective group,

have a higher propensity to have synesthesia. Now it makes sense when Jack described Aaron Neville as putting a lot of red in his music. Reports of such crossover perceptions have been confirmed by fMRI evidence, such as in activation of the color portion of the visual cortex in response to specific sounds.

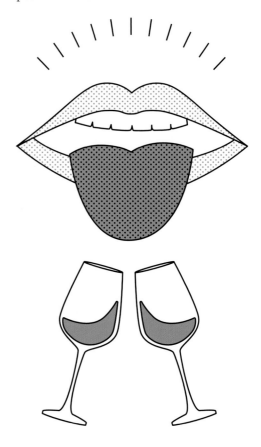

Scientists continue to uncover differences in our sensors (eyes, ears, nose, skin, tongue) and the pathways into the signal-processing centers of the brain. While the supertaster is an example of a genetic difference, learning can also boost sensory capabilities, which can be seen as a thickening of specific sensory-processing areas in brain scans. The wine connoisseur's expanded neural taste circuitry is learned through experience, as is a mother's sense of touch within her abdomen. This is why most moms can feel a second baby kick earlier than the first. We are evolving in our own lifetimes.

Then there are rats. The skull and crossbones, a universal symbol for poison, is highly recognizable. It doesn't take a connoisseur or

THOUGHT EXPERIMENT

HOW WOULD OUR BEHAVIORS CHANGE IF OUR LIVES WERE LIKE A MOVIE WE COULD REPLAY ANYWHERE, ANYTIME?

THOUGHT EXPERIMENT

IF YOU'RE LEAVING A FIRST IMPRESSION WITH A PROSPECTIVE CUSTOMER, HOW CLOSE CAN YOU GET TO A MOMENT WORTH CHASING FOR A LIFETIME?

supertaster to avoid poison with it on the label. It also doesn't require a human. Even lab rats can learn to recognize "logos" when it helps them avoid discomfort. Even rats get branding.

As brand owners seek to set up shop in our minds, we keep evolving and kicking out delinquent tenants. While it seems like hyperbole or scary science to think yourself into someone else's brain and check out what that person is sensing, our scientific understanding is advancing rapidly. And today we are advancing our ability to do this at an accelerating pace.

Around 400 B.C., Hippocrates theorized about the brain, "Through it, in particular, we think, see, hear, and distinguish the ugly from the beautiful, the bad from the good, the pleasant from the unpleasant." The brain's cellular processes were still largely unknown in 1949 when psychologist Donald Hebb hypothesized a mechanism for how neuronal circuits are modified to learn and create a memory. Now we evolve from navel gazing to gray matter gazing.

Years of "listening in" on individual animal neurons' firing in response to stimuli have enabled scientists to reverse engineer how some of the estimated 10,000 different types of neurons are involved in processing the signals received from our sensors. Studies of people with brain damage, experiments on animals' brains, and developments in diagnostic tools such as functional magnetic resonance imaging (fMRI) have helped map the physical location of specific processes within the brain. Converging this with the mapping of the human genome and deeper understanding of subcellular mechanisms is shedding new "light" on the processes of perception, attention, learning, and memory. More recent discoveries in a new discipline called optogenetics uses a benign virus to splice in a gene so that neurons react to light and can be made to fire on command using fiber optic threads in a living animal. Yeah, you have permission to be freaked out right about now.

The Human Genome Project cracked the code of our DNA in the 1990s. Similar ten-year efforts were launched in 2013 with the European Human Brain Project and the U.S. Brain Research

through Advancing Innovative Neurotechnologies (BRAIN) to further our understanding of the brain. From *MIT Technology Review*: "With the invention of optogenetics and other technologies, researchers can investigate the source of emotions, memory, and consciousness for the first time." We are at the edge of a Grand Canyon of knowledge and just about to look into the abyss.

When you combine all the many genetic differences in people with the diverse backgrounds none of us share, this idea of brands grouping "consumers" into categories like 18- to 34-year-old women is simplistic. The diversity of human genetics and backgrounds is amazing. For example, if everyone put this book down for two minutes, and then wrote three sentences about what they were thinking, none of those sentences would be the same.

FIT YOUR BRAIN FOR YOGA PANTS

MAKING SENSES

You probably thought that what you see, hear, and feel is exactly what reality is, even though you suspect that Vegas magician somehow hacked your brain. Instead, scientists now see that reality as we see it is literally a figment of our imagination. Our brain is designed to take shortcuts when possible to devote our processing resources to what matters for our survival.

For example, human sensory processes are designed to be acutely sensitive to changes in space and time. In vision, retinal neurons are biased toward detecting changes. These changes in light in a two-dimensional image reveal edges of objects. Edges that change quickly in time grab our attention such as lions, falling pianos, or video billboards. We are hardwired to act fast. It's a survival mechanism.

One shortfall to this visual system is that if there is no motion, retinal neurons stop firing. Apparently neurons have ADHD and are easily bored with the average visual inputs. To counter this, our eyes are constantly jittering to create a small high-frequency motion. If someone gave you a virtual reality helmet and matched the image movement to your eye movement, you'd be blind as a bat on a sunny afternoon. This is all the more reason for marketers to keep brand visual stimuli fresh.

The eyes can also be fooled by low-frequency motion. Slow changes in background objects in videos often go unnoticed and represent a type of optical illusion. Our inability to register slow changes in a scene is probably evolutionary. An approaching snail is unlikely to be a threat. In this sense, we are like frogs in slowly heating water. In the world of brands, this has been called "least noticeable change"; for example, our candy bars and burgers get smaller without anyone noticing, until someone does a historical time lapse.

For every 100 receptors in the eye, there is only one neuron reaching through the optic nerve into the brain. This means the retinal circuit must edit the visual information to convey what is most essential. So through the editing process your eyes are "seeing" more than what reaches your brain. Once information has passed into the brain, many other processing steps occur, and then your brain creates an internal model of external reality. We don't see the external world directly, and our conditioned beliefs, desires, and memories affect how we interpret what we see. We don't see the world as it is; we see it as we are.

The lower sensory processes unpack the information into fundamental elements such as color, contrast, orientation, and movement. These are inputs to intermediate processes, which identify object surfaces, foregrounds, and backgrounds. The high-level processes then match objects to memories to recognize them, place them into context, guide movement, learn, and evoke related memories. This is where it is helpful to know which fonts people recognize most quickly and what the current fashions are. Yes, neuroscientists study this stuff. Brand memories are stitched together from what we are experiencing and what we have experienced.

Within these processes, we use sensory data to create an initial interpretation and we fill in missing bits with predictions to create a mental representation. A classic example is our brain's ability to create a guess at what is in our blind spot. We don't notice that our sensory information is incomplete, which gives us a false sense of certainty and perhaps a better sense of security. It is little wonder that eyewitness accounts of crime scenes are so often wrong. For brands, there is an implication here that you don't need to tell the whole story, just the important bits.

Scientists and philosophers used to think we assemble a complete set of details into a precisely formed image. Instead, Immanuel Kant's Gestalt psychology seems to be born out by experimental data. That is, perception is part fact and part prediction. According to neuroscientist Charles Gilbert, "the brain guesses at the scene presented to the eyes based on past experience . . . The modern view is that perception is an active and creative process that involves more than just the information provided to the retina." And you thought just designers were creative. The hippies tripping on LSD were right: Perception is reality.

The study of our perceptual software bugs by scientists such as Nobel laureate Daniel Kahneman and by neuroscientist David Eagleman and others explains that the brain starts perception with a first approximation in our subconscious mind as an apparent way to economize on the conscious mind's focused attention. The conscious mind is recruited to handle surprises when apparent contradictions arise. Optical illusions are bugs even our conscious attention cannot easily resolve. All understanding is partial.

LET'S GET COLORFUL

BRAND EXPERIENCES IN TECHNICOLOR

Everything we've learned in our lives has come through our senses and the contents of our consciousness. Let's explore the sensory impact of some brand experiences and maybe apply some of our newfound neuroscience along the way.

We are only as capable as our senses; they offer the ability to advance and filter what we can consume and in what ways. So let's look into the senses, our portals to the outside world.

THOUGHT EXPERIMENT

WHAT WOULD THE SOUND OF CALM ORCHESTRAL MUSIC ADD TO THE AIRLINE BOARDING EXPERIENCE?

CHASING THE DRAGON

THE FIRST IS THE BEST CONTACT

While it might sound crazy, heroin subculture has something to teach a brand. The phrase "Chasing the dragon" is used to describe what often becomes a lifetime pursuit of the ultimate dopamine high. Now, while the culture surrounding this phrase has a rough underbelly, we can reappropriate the meaning. This first moment or best moments engaging with a brand can plant meaning more readily than the many so-so moments. This is why we believe there should be a carefully "designed" moment early and often in brand experience. Our senses are our portals to perception, the gateway to the mind.

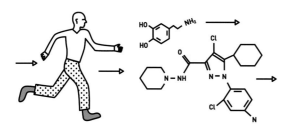

SEEING IS BELIEVING

OUR SENSE OF SIGHT

The eyes are gateways to perception, and perception is, as you now know, internal reality. Our eyes dominate our sensory perception by at least 5:1. Our brain dedicates more processing power to this sense over all others, yet it is the sense most likely to be fooled by visual trickery. We have learned that our eyes heavily edit incoming sensory data, and our beliefs and desires interpret what we see.

We are socially aware of the shortcomings of sight, yet we spend hard-earned income to be fooled. We even have an entire industry of "visual effects artists" specializing in fooling your eyes

for a living. Our eyes may be first to consume, but they are also first to be questioned. There are even specialists to study how we perceive colors, human faces, and what things we are likely to remember because of the visual images in our minds. We can miss unusual events and see things that did not happen. Seeing is believing, they say, but then again, who are "they" and do you really believe them?

We also consume information with our visual perception and make judgments before we read. This is why there are terms like "visual language" or symbols. Words and pictures are symbols. Visual communication and judgment happens before a message is read. We see this in our world when kids are able to identify a brand, remember it, and say it back to us before they are able to read. This suggests that visual symbols should be well aligned with written or spoken language. Customers intuitively pick up on inconsistencies and may not be able to articulate what's actually inconsistent with the visual communication. Visual and verbal consistency is a proxy for consistent brand quality.

The other challenge with sight is brand blindness. Some brands have achieved such ubiquity in our lives that we become blind to their presence. Brands lawyers would classify as "superbrands" that achieve 100 percent unaided awareness can be on the receiving end of 100 percent social blindness. These brands are present in our lives; we purchase them with a pattern of loyalty, but we don't even see them anymore. Coca-Cola has achieved this distinction, which they recognized after asking random fans exiting the Coca-Cola stadium in Atlanta, "Who was the primary sponsor of this event?" They found an extremely small percentage of fans even noticed the Coca-Cola brand. The brand became wallpaper in a highly cluttered room, hidden by all the other messages bombarding the attendees at this event. This is why brands like Coca-Cola are constantly searching for new meaning, new relevance. Familiarity can breed apathy, so sometimes big brands need to break the mold they've formed in our heads, without breaking our coveted mental images.

Brand blindness has a big impact on the global community of brands trying to communicate across cultures and language barriers. We make statements like "people just don't read anymore," yet have entire movements around the phrase "content is king" and the concept of "content marketing" as a modern method to engage "consumers." These seem diametrically opposed. Yet the common thread just requires closer examination. Here's a comparison to help clarify the differences.

A single seventeenth-century Englishman was exposed to as much information in his lifetime as we have packed into a daily edition of the *New York Times* newspaper, though few human beings in the modern world have actually read every word of an entire *New York Times* newspaper. But consider how much reading we do in a lifetime compared to a typical seventeenth-century person. So, in fact, we read more today than we ever have, but we're more selective. Reading material and the ability to read was rather limited before Gutenberg's invention. Today we've got more than enough to read, so we're careful what we consume. By the way, thanks for choosing to read this sentence. We appreciate it.

BEAUTY IS NOT A POKE IN THE EYE

THE GOOD, TRUE, TRULY BEAUTIFUL

We are attracted to beauty from the moment we open our eyes. This much is known. The measurement of beauty is less known. Yet the measurements of beauty are used all around us; we just don't see the math. Going back to ancient Greece, Aristotle saw that persuasion could be accomplished through beauty, truth, and morality—and the progressive thinker Pythagoras is credited for inventing a musical scale that connected the beauty of music with the physical world and mathematics. Who knows, perhaps Socrates would not have been forced to drink hemlock for his commitment to truth had he been more handsome.

Somehow these Greek polymaths also stumbled upon a mathematical formula for beauty. It's called the golden mean, golden ratio, or the Fibonacci sequence, and is represented by the Greek letter phi. Some say that this simple ratio of 1.618 to 1 led to the design of the Parthenon, and today, some contemporary designers use it as a central rubric when designing. The golden ratio has since been proven as an ideal ratio for beautiful proportion. Amazingly, most of architecture, graphic, product, and advertising design have this ratio built in. So while you may not see faces everywhere, the beauty we see in faces is mathematically embedded everywhere. Your eyes have been consuming beauty far beyond the last runway fashion show.

OUR SENSE OF SOUND

We hear much, listen less. For one thing, the other senses are always clamoring for attention. So is that ever-present voice inside our heads. Then there is the challenge of establishing common meaning through language, which is not easy because every one of these words is a figment of your imagination and proxy for auditory signals, interpreted through your current context in space and time. If we have not confused you enough, let's get into the mechanics of our miraculous auditory organs.

Sound is a vibration in physics—a mechanical wave of pressure like a wave in the ocean. We consume sound physiologically, through our ears and the rest of our body. When we say a song touches us, the truth is it actually does touch us in a physical way, with waves of sound. This interaction with the sense of touch is partly why sound helps form an emotional bond. Consider mosh pits in a punk rock concert.

There are experiments where the background music in movies changes between clips, altering how it changes a scene. The emotional impact on the state of the viewer is profound. While many brands would acknowledge sound is second to sight, this doesn't explain the whole story. Brands using sound actually use touch as well, which is why we can't really compartmentalize

the five senses (more on touch later). They all intermingle in ways that are only partially understood. If you've been in the world of marketing and consider sound an important part of your sensory mix, the first leap might be to radio, broadcast media, or online video. These can't actually be measured against other mediums in a digital economy.

Sound has a profound impact on our brand experiences. Compare a typical restaurant today to fifty years ago. In the past, the removal of sound was standard; most popular restaurants would be quiet to allow for conversation. They were the places to be seen, but not heard. Today, the dull roar of a restaurant is an unspoken indication of popularity. Just try to have a quiet conversation in the most popular restaurant in your city. Sound is both a blunt instrument and a subtle indicator of a brand's social popularity. And to put a fine line on the connections between sound and touch, consider that many restaurants use fast-tempo music timed to heartbeats to create anxiety and turn their tables faster.

THE BEAUTIFUL SOUND OF SILENCE

HEARING MORE EXAMPLES

In order to really talk about sound, we need you to perform a small "listen for the quiet" experiment first. Find the busiest place in close proximity, go there, and close your eyes. Well, first read this next line and then close them and count to sixty.

What did you hear? Make a list of the sounds you heard or speak them back to yourself. Describe them as best you can. Can you identify any brands you've heard? Now imagine a day listening to the sounds in your life. Where do you interact with sounds the most often? What sounds do you hear almost every day? Can you identify any brands based on sound alone? Some brands already believe this is possible and worthy of seeking trademark protection.

Here are some examples; some are common, others less so.

- INTEL HAS A TRADEMARKED SOUND YOU'VE MOST LIKELY HEARD IF YOU'VE WATCHED BROADCAST TELEVISION IN THE PAST DECADE. SINCE INTEL IS AN INGREDIENT BRAND INSIDE OTHER TECHNOLOGY, IT'S LOGICAL FOR IT TO FIND OTHER SENSORY IMPACT OUTSIDE THE BEIGE BOXES KNOWN AS COMPUTERS AT THE TIME.

- APPLE HAS A TRADEMARK SOUND FOR THE START UP OF A MAC COMPUTER, WHICH, FOR THEIR AUDIENCES, HAS LIKELY MADE MANY MORE IMPRESSIONS THAN THE BROADCAST ADVERTISING OF THE INTEL SOUND. APPLE ALSO HAS A PATENT FOR AN AIRPLANE ICON THAT ACCOMPANIES ITS DISTINCTIVE AIRPLANE SOUND WHEN YOU SEND AN E-MAIL FROM A PHONE.

- HARLEY-DAVIDSON ATTEMPTED TO TRADEMARK THEIR ENGINE SOUND, BUT FOUND THEMSELVES ROAD BLOCKED BY ALL THE OTHER MOTORCYCLE BRANDS. LEGO ATTEMPTED TO TRADEMARK THE CLICK OF THEIR BLOCKS ATTACHING, BUT ALSO DIDN'T FIND A PATH TO LEGAL PROTECTION.

These examples provide us with a perspective on the future of what might be important to brands. The sounds associated with brands show up in a variety of places, and brand teams are realizing the importance of protecting a sound that has achieved distinctiveness.

Culturally, does this mean we will hear more use of sound in the design of brand experiences? Likely. You can't shut out sound easily versus sight, where you can close your eyes to turn off input. Sound actually enters your body and touches you, so the emotional impact can be dramatic for a brand owner. Many brands just don't consider sound as a part of their experience, but as knowledge of the impact of sound grows, more will adopt it.

REACH IN AND TOUCH SOMEONE

OUR SENSE OF TOUCH

Touch is the easiest of the five senses to miss, and one we could not live without. The sense should not be reserved for the product design team (touching a physical product) and the sales team (handshake and slap on the back) inside most organizations. Touch is the sense interacting with our largest organ, 21 square feet of space on our bodies: our skin. From lying on a bed, sitting in a chair, to the simplicity of a proper handshake, touch is a highly personal sense. Touch can bond someone with a brand if you're willing to break the barrier or thoughtfully design opportunities for touch.

Just in the past decade or so, the hotel industry has realized that the mattress and pillow are critical to their coveted business travelers. If you're wondering why this wasn't figured out until the year 2000, we wondered this, too. The experience of a hotel peaks with a wonderful night's sleep, and research shows the bed is a primary consideration for frequent travelers. If you've traveled for business, you know how a change in mattress, pillow, and surrounding sounds can help or hinder sleep. The sense of touch in this experience can lead to deep sleep and deep loyalty. According to the *Hotel Managers Group Blog*, "Hotels are more likely to attract and retain loyal guests by improving guest experiences. Visitors will respond better to comfortable mattresses and extra fancy linens than they will to a free basic breakfast buffet."

DESIGN AND ENVIRONMENTAL SCIENCE GOT MARRIED

THE METHOD HOME MOVEMENT

In San Francisco, Eric Ryan and Adam Lowry started Method, a brand of naturally derived, biodegradable, nontoxic household cleaners, laundry supplies, personal care, and soap, when green cleaning products didn't have the reputation for being effective at, well, cleaning. "Back in 2001, green cleaners were just hideous looking," Ryan says, "and the conventional wisdom was that green didn't clean." Thank you *Slate Magazine* and Mr. Ryan.

Method's advertising efforts have been more of a movement than a campaign. Method started by taking on the large established brands that had centuries of combined history (Procter & Gamble, Johnson & Johnson, Clorox). The Method team was bold, but they saw a better way to clean and a better way to do business.

These two lifelong friends took on two challenges at once: redesign of the cleaning category and the effectiveness of environmentally responsible cleaning. Lowry, with a degree in chemical engineering and a background in environmental science, formulated a dish soap and a line of all-purpose cleaners that were nontoxic and biodegradable. Ryan has an eye for design from working at Gap, Fallon, and Saturn, so he could see sleek, elegant containers. Hiring industrial designer Karim Rashid helped Method seal a distribution deal with Target. From there, Method unveiled hand soap in the brand's iconic teardrop-shaped bottle. Eric also hung a banner over their movement by calling it "People Against Dirty."

This movement approach to building a brand has shown it is possible to run a financially successful green business and do it with minimal traditional advertising. Method was named the seventh-fastest-growing private company in the country in 2006 by *Inc.* magazine. And Method now has some new friends in the green-clean category.

Recently, Method set its sights on reinventing laundry detergent and launched a triple-concentrated, biodegradable formula that's dispensed by a pump. The pump interface helps people keep to the proper amount of detergent for a high-efficiency washer. This authentic approach earned Method a Very Innovative Product award from *Good Housekeeping.* Eric and Adam aim to make Method manufacturing, packaging, and distribution processes as earth-friendly as possible by using nontoxic, locally sourced product ingredients and shipping in biodiesel-fueled trucks.

As a multisensory example, Method was required to take a distinctive route to market in order to achieve success. Let's consider a leading competitor, the hand soap container for Softsoap owned by Colgate-Palmolive. The design intention of Softsoap is focused on selling loudly at the retail shelf with far less concern for where this container would be displayed in a typical household. The Method teardrop vessel was designed to fit nicely in a designed bathroom and set itself apart from a cluttered (visually loud) shelf space at Target.

This kind of thinking isn't accidental; it is a "design thinking" approach to understanding the relationship people have with cleaning products. Having empathy for the person and his individual context is a contrast with considering the selling environment (Target in this case) first. The outcome from Method's approach is a visually appealing design for the Target shopper buying Method and their houseguests (community). Couple this with the unique scents used to distinguish the brand and the feel of the containers in your hand and Eric and Adam designed a multisensory moment. Perhaps you've had this moment, the first time when you enter a friend's house with the Method teardrop proudly displayed in the main floor loo.

All these efforts make for socially shareable stories, good feelings, media coverage, and a product experience that is designed to earn loyalty. Purpose has trumped promotion with this method, pun intended.

WHEN WERE YOU LAST TOUCHED? UNKNOWN

CONCLUDING MEMORIES

THE BOUNDARY BETWEEN WHAT WE DO AND DO NOT KNOW ABOUT THE HUMAN BRAIN IS RAPIDLY DIMINISHING, THOUGH THERE ARE STILL SUBSTANTIAL AREAS THAT REMAIN UNKNOWN. ADVANCES IN OPTOGENETICS AND OTHER RESEARCH METHODS, ALONG WITH AGGRESSIVE FUNDING FOR BRAIN RESEARCH, ARE EXPECTED TO EXPAND OUR UNDERSTANDING OF HOW MEMORIES ARE FORMED FROM SENSORY INPUT. THIS IS DIRECTLY RELEVANT TO BRAND BUILDING AND MANAGEMENT IN SEVERAL WAYS:

1 Our brain filters the many signals that we receive every day and does not process all signals in the same way. The vast majority of these signals are ignored.

2 We all react differently to signals we receive, especially people like supertasters, but we all notice changes to signals in our physical environment. Logos and recognizable symbols help us to process brands more quickly.

3 Each of our senses helps build brand awareness. Sight and sound are the most common, but touch, smell, and taste can leave more lasting impressions.

4 Diverse sensory perceptions predispose different people toward different brands. Market segmentation is, at least in part, a process of discovering subpopulations with common brain functionality.

06

MOMENTS + MEMORY

MOMENTS AND MEMORIES, MOMENTS AND MEMORIES,
MOMENTS AND MEMORIES—REPEAT IT TEN TIMES TO
EMBED THE PATTERN AND CREATE A BRAND. BE SURE
TO GIVE YOURSELF A MOMENT TO LET THE SIGNALS STICK.
YOU ARE ABOUT TO EXPLORE TYPES AND FORMS OF
MEMORIES AND HOW MEMORIES ARE STORED IN THE BRAIN.
YOU'LL LEARN MORE ABOUT THE MANY ROUGH ROADS TO
LEARNING, AND HOW THE MILKY WAY IN YOUR HEAD IS
CAPABLE OF STORING AND WARPING LONG-TERM MEMORIES.
THEN, IF MEMORY STORAGE ISN'T HARD ENOUGH, YOU'LL
LEARN ABOUT THE HALF-LIFE OF A MEMORY, WHICH MAY
LEAVE YOU WONDERING WHY ANYONE TAKES UP THE
CHALLENGE OF BUILDING A BRAND IN THE FIRST PLACE.
BUT AS YOU WILL LEARN LATER, THE REWARDS CAN BE
WORTH THE EFFORT, MANY TIMES OVER.

WHEN SENSORY SIGNALS STICK

ALL ABOUT MOMENTS AND MEMORY

So we've already established that we are overwhelmed with sensory signals every day, that most of these signals never make it to the brain, and that your brain concocts an artificial version of external reality. The big question then is how do brands make memories? Our answer: moments in time and space that are emotionally compelling and ideally multisensory. Some people are hardwired to fully appreciate your brand moments; others are not. That's okay as long as you have more appreciators than haters.

Memories live and fade in neurons, the inner space where the contest for brand supremacy is fought. The more we know about neurons, the more we learn that they operate in predictable, but hard to measure, ways. This has led many philosophers including Daniel Dennett to conclude free will is limited, while hard determinists see human behavior as nothing more than ongoing chain reactions of cause and effect. These ideas could explain why some brands somehow seem to be able to crack the cipher and embed themselves in our memories with the right signals. If this paragraph is starting to feel like you are living inside the movie *The Matrix*, don't worry, just "take the blue pill."

There are an estimated 86 billion neurons in your brain with over 10,000 connections from each neuron extending to other neurons. So if one of your neurons (let's call him Bob) had a Facebook account, he would only be separated by two other neurons from anyone else on earth (including Kevin Bacon). Brand energy lives in gray matter, which stores memories, and white matter, which connects memories and ideas between different parts of the brain. White matter is like the freeways between counties, and the county roads run in gray matter.

The good news is that you only have to succeed in laying one durable path of long-term memory to gain recall. The better news is that you don't have to have all of your eggs in one basket. Multiple memory paths from multisensory experiences improve your odds of reaching long-term memory and reinforce each other for a stronger total recall.

All of this brain science will give you a better understanding of how brands operate in the brain. It is important to remember that science seems to open an infinite matryoshka doll, where each new answer leads to another confounding question. We'll never know it all. As Herb Kelleher, founder and CEO of Southwest Airlines, said, "Sure, we have a strategic plan. It's called doing things." This philosophy seems to have worked well for Herb and Southwest. Let's move along now and take a look at how brand moments turn into long-term memories.

YOU FORGOT YOUR FLASH DRIVE

MEMORY TYPES AND PROCESSES

Several types of memories are stored in different places within the brain, connected by white matter. These types of memory can work alone or in tandem, and can interact with each other when necessary. For example, a novice golfer would use her conscious focus to follow step-by-step directions under the guidance of an instructor for her first golf swing. The step-by-step directions would initially be stored in explicit (conscious) memory. Repetition of the swing begins the path to lay down implicit (subconscious) muscle memory. Eventually, implicit memory developed through practice by an experienced golfer is best left alone by the conscious mind. Overthinking the process can mess up a good swing.

The primary memory processes for each type of memory include encoding, storage, consolidation, and retrieval. While these processes can occur solo in a single memory type, the previous examples illustrate the benefits of interactions between different memory types when encoding and retrieving memories. This could be why multisensory experiences over time tend to create strong brands. Eventually, purchases become implicit habits not easily broken.

SEMANTIC VS. EPISODIC MEMORY

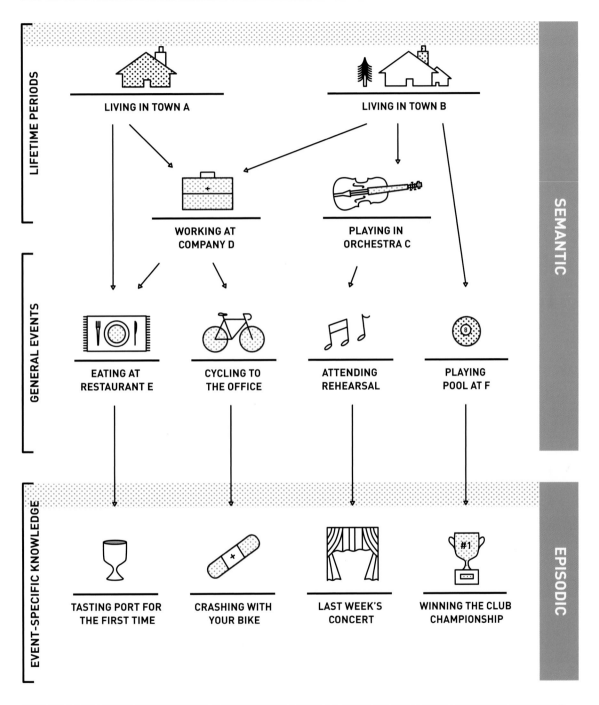

EPISODIC MEMORIES OF REPEATED EXPERIENCES ACCUMULATE INTO SEMANTIC MEMORIES OVER TIME. ONLY STANDOUT MOMENTS REMAIN AS DISTINCT EPISODIC MEMORIES. (ADAPTED FROM THE DOCTORAL THESIS OF JOHAN WILLANDER, STOCKHOLM UNIVERSITY, 2007.)

HONEY, PLEASE COME DRAW IN BED

EXPLICIT MEMORIES

There are two forms of conscious and explicit memory: episodic and semantic. Episodic memories are events in our life that are most closely tied to "the self" and guides what most people consider to be a memory. Semantic memories provide conscious access to objects and facts. These are abstract concepts (a.k.a. memes) assembled over time from our episodic experiences. Take, for example, the concept of a bed. From a first crib to a big-boy bed, to Mommy and Daddy's bed, to a waterbed, to a college dorm bed, to that first apartment bed, or, finally, to an adjustable air mattress platform bed—people develop their own generic concept that comes to mind with the word *bed*.

If asked to think of a bed, people can retrieve their semantic memory concept of "bed" faster than they can the specific "my bed" they woke from that morning. When asked to draw "my bed" they might start with one detail such as the headboard, but still draw the semantic "bed" legs. Further prompting might allow them to provide detail for "my bed's" legs. So the more examples we have to work with surrounding an object memory, the less specific we are with our recall. As an industry or category gets more congested, it is harder for people to distinguish brands in memory.

SEW WHAT?

A MOMENT STORED

As a brand owner, would you prefer people to access their memories of your product from semantic memory or episodic memory? Where do you think the word *Kleenex* is stored in your brain? If it defines a product category, it would represent the semantic object and would be top of mind in unaided retail (not a bad position to

be in if you weren't concerned about losing your legal rights to enforce your trademark). If *Kleenex* resided in episodic memory as the brand your mother always bought, it might take longer for the memory to be retrieved, but have stronger legal protection.

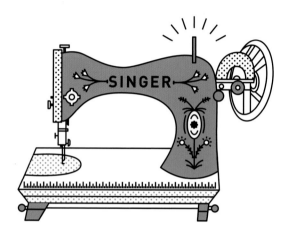

Too much brand success can lead to failure. Ironies are all around us. Just ask the companies that launched and later lost their legal rights to the brands yo-yo, aspirin, cellophane, thermos, escalator, dry ice, trampoline, and the word *Webster* to mean dictionary.

In 1896, half a century after its launch, the Singer sewing machine was so prominent that the name was used by the public to describe a general class of home sewing machine. Competitors used the name to describe their products (a "June singer"). The U.S. Supreme Court ruled that *Singer* had become a generic term and that the Singer Manufacturing Company no longer had rights to its exclusive use. Another half-century later, the U.S. Fifth Circuit Court of Appeals decided that Singer had regained its rights to the exclusive use of the name because public use of the name had come to once again indicate just the products sold by Singer Manufacturing Company (now

Singer Corporation). Unfortunately, the product class had become nearly obsolete by then, so the reacquired rights were a sort of bubblegum prize. The public perception and therefore memories determine the brand owner's rights. The owner can only hope to guide, advance, and protect these memories.

Google's rights to its name have been challenged repeatedly in courts claiming genericide, a brand equivalent to an international war crime. Forbes estimates the Google brand has a value of $66 billion, the third most valuable brand in the world behind Apple and Microsoft. According to Forbes, Google has so far succeeded in keeping its rights in court cases, but, like Kleenex and Xerox, has had to keep a constant vigil and regularly retain lawyers to keep the full benefits of its branding success. In August of 2015, the Google brand's owner took a further step to protect its rights to the Google name by changing its corporate name from Google to Alphabet.

Yes, this is a tree falling in the woods kind of thought experiment, but still worth pondering. Perhaps if your brand is buried into the semantic object memory of "a bed is a bed is a bed," but no longer stands out as unique, they might buy your product if you have the lowest price or by random choice. However, this is unlikely to be profit maximizing. If your product lacks additional customer utility, your brand would have minimal potential value.

If there exists a subset of people more apt to enjoy your brand over others because of their sensory wiring, you might find them (or they might find you). You can increase the odds of planting an episodic memory through customer experience by offering a free trial, by presenting an appealing package, or designing an experiential "moment." If you are looking to form an explicit memory with a brand launch through national brand advertising, the odds of swimming upstream into long-term memory are so against you, even Vegas casinos would be embarrassed to take your money. However, if the ad leads to a sale, you win the jackpot!

WORKING MEMORY AND EXPLICIT MEMORY

Explicit memory starts with working memory. Working memory resides in one of the newest and most humanly evolutionary additions to our brains, the prefrontal cortex, which is likely getting a good workout in this chapter. Although the prefrontal cortex has tremendous advantages, it is unfortunately underpowered, distracted, and diminished with stress.

Working memory contains special neurons that stay on while waiting to be transferred into a more stable form of memory. When new stimulus is received, working memory loses focus and moves on to new information. Think of pressing a key on an organ, which stays on until you stop pressing the key, versus a piano key, which fades over time, even if you keep on pressing the key. Working memory acts like organ keys; neurons in long-term memory act like piano keys.

As an example of working memory, if someone tells you her Twitter handle while you are distracted by a vibrating message on your Apple Watch before you can commit it to long-term memory, it will be lost forever. And, we know, there doesn't have to be much commotion to distract us today. This is why when a waitperson doesn't write down your lunch order and he gets it right, you should tip him a bit more than 15 percent. Attention is a scarce resource and screens are all around us.

WE'RE LYING TO OURSELVES

TYPES OF MEMORY

If you've spent time with people, asking them questions in context of a purchase, you've run into the common truth that people lie to researchers. They will say, "I only buy healthy options for my family," while grasping a basket full of Doritos, mac 'n' cheese, and diet cola. What you don't

THOUGHT EXPERIMENT

IF YOUR BRAND IS IN A PERSON'S SEMANTIC MEMORY, BUT NOT IN EPISODIC MEMORY, WOULD HE STILL FIND YOU?

WHERE IN THE WORLD IS . . . YOUR MEMORY?

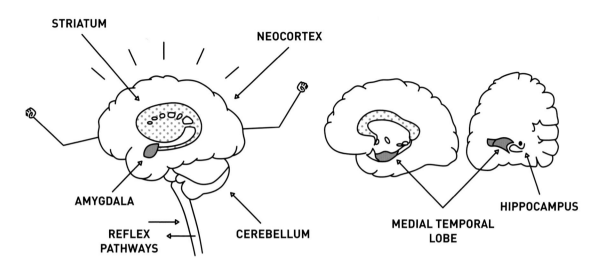

LOOKING AT YOUR BRAIN IS LIKE WATCHING YOURSELF ON VIDEO — ALWAYS A BIT AWKWARD. KNOWING WHERE YOUR AMYGDALA IS RELATIVE TO YOUR HIPPOCAMPUS WILL NOT HELP FIND AN ACTUAL MEMORY, BUT IT MAY HELP FORM A NEW MEMORY ABOUT HOW POWERFUL AND IMPORTANT THESE SMALL PARTS OF YOUR BRAIN ARE. IT MAY ALSO HELP KEEP YOU FROM SCRATCHING YOUR NOGGIN WHILE YOU'RE READING THIS SECTION.

realize is they actually lie to themselves as well. There's an explanation in our memory about why this happens.

There are three primary categories of implicit or subconscious memory: (A) Habits and Skills (motor and perceptual), (B) Priming, and (C) Conditioning (classical and operant). Because implicit memories are subconscious, they cannot be accessed directly with the conscious mind, making market research difficult. Although we can direct the training of implicit memory through conscious acts of repetition, we cannot necessarily explain how or why that training works. More research is needed on the involvement of implicit memories when brands are creating multisensory experiences across time and space.

According to neuroscientist David Eagleman, "We have ways of retrospectively telling stories about our actions as though the actions were always our idea." In his book *Incognito: The Secret Lives of the Brain* he explains that people who have

had the two hemispheres of their brains surgically disconnected to prevent life-threatening seizures sometimes find themselves literally with two minds. For example, a person with a split brain may enjoy a novel if she holds it in her right hand, but if she holds it in her left hand she will get bored, because the right brain controls the left hand and cannot read.

If you still believe everything people in focus groups tell you about your brand, maybe you should think it through a bit more with the organ between your ears. Our conscious self cannot explain any customer choice originating from implicit memory. However, rather than admitting our lack of insight into our actions, we make up a story. This is why focus groups and surveys often fail to predict customer choice—they are asking the wrong part of the brain, a part of the brain that can't talk. This is why behaviors scream louder than words and we, as marketers, often don't listen. These behaviors don't fit our construct of what "should" happen.

SO EASY EVEN A RAT CAN DO IT

EXPERIMENT ONE

explicit learning

EXPERIMENT TWO

implicit learning

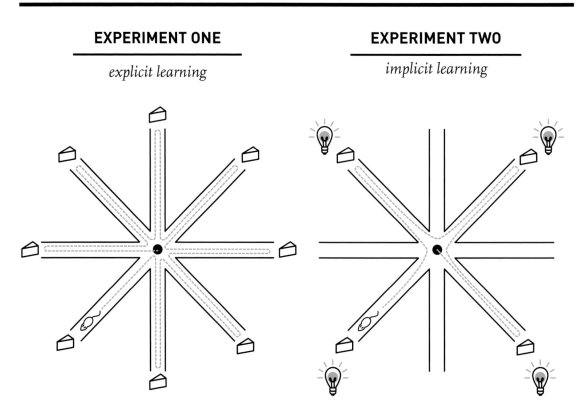

SOMETIMES LIFE FEELS THIS WAY WHEN YOU'RE LOOKING FOR A GOOD CUP OF COFFEE. JUST LOOK FOR THE STARBUCKS LOGO—A BEACON ON THE HORIZON. LOGOS ARE LANGUAGE, AND EVEN WITHOUT READING WE'RE LEARNING. CONSIDER THAT THE NEXT TIME YOU PICK COMIC SANS FOR YOUR TYPEFACE.

TWO DIRT ROADS TO LEARNING

PATHS TO LEARNING

According to neuroscientist Charles Gilbert, "Many habits are learned early and retained throughout life. We learn to navigate through the world without conscious thought." Although habits can appear to draw from explicit (conscious) memory, these two kinds of memory are stored and operate explicitly and implicitly, or consciously and subconsciously.

In two different experiments, scientists studied rats in a maze with tunnels projecting as spokes from a central platform. At the end of each spoke, there may or may not be food.

In one experiment, the rats had to go down each tunnel only once to get the food, so they had to remember which tunnels they had already gone down. This task relied upon explicit memory. In the other experiment, they had to learn that the lighted tunnels had food. This learning to associate light with food relies on the habit type of implicit memory and involves a different pathway in the brain. Researchers confirmed that these are entirely independent forms of memory. Surgically impairing one of the two paths did nothing to hinder learning in the other and vice versa.

How many of our purchases are done out of habit? It is estimated that 95 percent of human behavior is following an existing habit. But only 9 percent of marketers are aware of this daunting statistic. Pause and consider that meaty statistic for a moment. Now when did you last take the time to evaluate different toothpastes in the grocery store and actually read the entire package? Many of these habits are left unbroken by competitors. But with sampling and free trial experiences, habits can be broken and new ones formed.

Now let's train people to form a habit of purchasing a brand. Motor skills are, as was already discussed, muscle memory. They can also include seemingly higher-level functions that can be performed on autopilot while our conscious attention is focused elsewhere. For example, people who are asked to recognize mirror images of letters initially use their conscious learning capabilities to perform this task. In an fMRI, this is seen as activated higher visual processing functions. After many repetitions, those abilities go nearly silent as sight-driven habits take over. In your brain, this is just to the right of the Golden Arches and due south of your beautiful and simple logo. Neurons that fire together wire together. Repetition is the key.

If packaging and fonts of all products looked the same, we would have to read words on a box to find our favorite brand. Images travel much, much faster. Reading requires the burdensome use of conscious attention, so thanks for sticking with us here. How much time out of each day would we lose if we couldn't delegate to our subconscious? Grocery shopping would take on a whole new degree of annoyance.

Priming is a related form of implicit memory in which an image or fact can be recognized, increasing the speed of access to explicit memories. A successful logo taps into this ability to aid recall, even when it is partially obscured. A few notes from a memorable advertising jingle or a corner of a logo can launch an explicit memory through priming. While this would imply "make our logo bigger" should be said more often, it is important to clarify: Just because it's bigger doesn't make it more visible or recognizable. People don't like a pushy salesperson or egomaniac yelling at them.

YOUR BODY KNOWS

CLASSICAL AND OPERANT CONDITIONING

Classical conditioning (think Pavlov and his dogs) is an association between two or more stimuli where one is benign (the ringing bell) and the other is strong (reward or pain). Operant conditioning is the association of action with outcome, such as pushing a lever to get food. Most conditioning requires cause and effect to occur in a short period.

A big exception to the short interval is that people will often avoid a food if they end up sitting on the white throne several hours after it was eaten. This makes evolutionary sense. It takes time for food poisoning to work its magic. However, this is unique to the sense of taste. If a sound or image is followed by nausea several hours later, nothing will happen. Likewise, if stomach pain follows the consumption of food, but no nausea, we won't connect the dots. The challenge for brands is to avoid negative conditioning and increase positive conditioning. If you've enjoyed an Uber experience and then endured a terrible taxi ride in the same day, you now know why the taxi trade is in deep trouble.

BIOGRAPHY AND BIOLOGY DANCING TOGETHER

EVOLVING IN OUR LIFETIME

Neuroplasticity is the newest rage. It used to be thought that we were born with a life's supply of neurons and that they were already hardwired into the design of Human version 1.0. Instead, we see the brain's amazing ability to rewire in response to learning, experiences, and social interactions that redeploy neurons around damaged areas. We add circuitry when we learn to play a musical instrument or meditate. We lose circuitry when we stop using certain functions or stop mentally visiting memories. We are continuously evolving into version 2.0 of our old selves. This fact opens

A REFRESHER FROM PSYCH 101

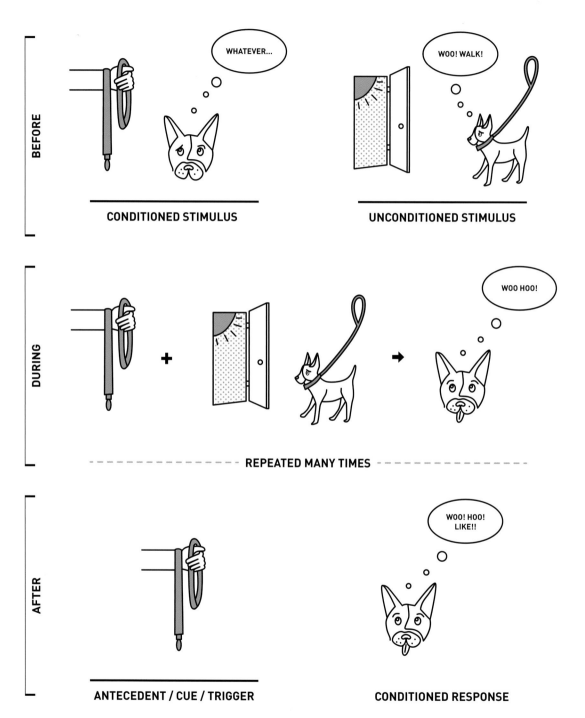

THIS IS FOR THOSE WHO NAMED THEIR DOG PAVLOV AND CAN ENJOY THE IRONY OF A DOG WALK.
IN CLASSICAL CONDITIONING, WE ARE THE DOG AND THE BRAND OWNER IS HOLDING THE LEASH.
YET, FOR MODERN DOG OWNERS, FIDO HAS CONDITIONED THE OWNER TO FEED HIM, LET HIM OUT, AND
THE BEST PART, PICK UP THE PILES HE LEAVES BEHIND.

the door for new brands to groove new neural networks and unseat old ones.

Donald Hebb's 1949 hypothesis that we create and strengthen neuronal synaptic connections as we learn has been borne out in experiments. Along the way, scientists have discovered the anti-Hebbian phenomenon of the pruning and weakening of connections when they are left unused for long periods. Relying on a smartphone or GPS navigation will shrink areas of your hippocampus. Since most of us are no longer using our internal spatial navigation system to find our way in the world, neurons in that part of the brain prune connections. Use it or lose it. Skeptical? Try going without your mapping device of choice the next time you're heading toward an unknown destination. You'll feel something missing—parts of your brain, to be exact.

Meanwhile, inventor and futurist Ray Kurzweil's projection of transferring his own neural network into a computer is getting closer than we know. As computing devices increasingly take the place of human brain processes, will we lose those processes until we are no longer needed? Kurzweil says it won't matter much, because by 2025 we'll all carry computers that are as smart as we are to take care of the details in life.

THE ENDS OF THE EMOTIONAL SPECTRUM

MEMORABLE EXPERIENCES

How far down the rabbit hole of memory do you want to go? The more you know, the better you can understand human behavior and memories. Neuroscientists are generally confident that all mental activities are physical. For example, mental illnesses are either due to brain structural abnormalities or may be abnormalities that occur solely at the cellular and molecular level. A corollary discovery is that explicit and implicit memory processes utilize similar cellular and molecular building blocks even though they function in different parts of the brain. Learning about the brain is like unpeeling an endless artichoke. Think about this next time you think a big communication idea alone will make a sale.

And then it gets even deeper. Our human experiences can lead to long-term changes in cellular genetic expression (called epigenetic changes) and can play an important role in learning, memory, and behavior. Some epigenetic changes follow a traumatic experience and result in amplified synaptic responses to certain stimuli, such as in post-traumatic stress disorder (PTSD). Some epigenetic changes can be passed to the next generation. So if you had a horrid food poisoning experience at a Howard Johnson's restaurant as a child, you might pass that down to your kids, genetically. And if you're a brand owner, the extremes of the emotional spectrum are more likely to have a memorable impact.

The formation of an explicit memory and its ultimate storage as long-term memory begins with the working memory, "organ key" neurons that retain information for just a few minutes. From there, neurons transfer the information to other neurons in the medial temporal lobe and its hippocampal structure, and after about a week, these memories can live in the cerebral cortex. This process is somewhat like stringing new electrical wiring through your brain. When it's done, you can flip the switch to send energy down the wire and the light will turn on to illuminate the memory. Even if it's been months or years since you strung that wire, the light might still work. As time progresses, though, you risk having a mouse chew through the line, and by then it'll be too late to call an electrician. If you only laid one line, you're out of luck. That memory is gone and your brand is diminished. That's why smart brands seek to connect through multiple sensory channels.

A MILKY WAY OF CONNECTIONS IN YOUR HEAD

OUR CAPACITY FOR MEMORY

Neurons are highly interconnected, with each neuron having as many as 10,000 synaptic connections to other neurons, and there are about 86 billion neurons. This high connectivity gives it massive computing power, with the same neuron playing a role in multiple memories. Scientists believe the memory storage potential for this system is effectively limitless. We are limited only in our ability to encode and retrieve memories.

Dr. John O'Keefe was awarded a Nobel Prize in 2014 for his 1971 discovery of place cells in the mouse hippocampus and their role in remembering spatial information. According to neuroscientists Eric Kandel and Steven Siegelbaum, "When the animal enters a new environment, new 'place fields' are formed within minutes and are stable for weeks to months. Thus, if one records the electrical activity of a number of place cells it is possible to predict where the animal is in its environment. In this manner the hippocampus is thought to constitute a cognitive map of the animal's surroundings." A later discovery identified other hippocampal cells that contain a sort of spatial grid of memory. Place cells with details about a place in the grid are mapped to a position in the grid through neural connections. Neuroscientist John O'Keefe describes the spatial memory system further: "Spatial cells found in the hippocampal formation represent the animal's location (place cells), its current heading direction (head direction cells), the metric of the environment (grid cells), and the animal's distance from boundaries of the environment (boundary vector cells)."

Place cells are intriguing because they reveal what seems to be a sequential "writing" of new information into neurons to record new surroundings, analogous to the recording of a new song on a phonographic record or a hard drive. By the way, the rats in O'Keefe's experiment had only graphic patterns on the wall as a guide to where they were in the maze. The place cells were associated with the mouse's memory of each of the patterns so that the patterns could guide them through the maze. A grocery store is the human counterpart to O'Keefe's maze, as we use logos to guide our way through the aisles (and you thought logos were only for human consumption).

These discoveries also indicate how the amygdala encodes memories in a similar cellular mechanisms used by the hippocampus, although the amygdala specializes in conditional learning of emotional responses. Likewise, other memory factories reside in other parts of the brain, wired together with white matter. The more brain systems a brand touches, the more routes to explicit and implicit memory.

RAISING A CROP OF BINDING PROTEINS

LONG-TERM MEMORIES FIND A HOME

Just when your brain is gasping for air, we're going deeper into cellular details to see how new synaptic connections are formed. It is a whole other world of wonder and complexity.

Consider a brain experiencing its first "moment" with your brand. Inside the brain, working memory neurons turn on like an expansive organ chord from Bach's Toccata and Fugue in D-Minor. They set off a series of firings jumping from neuron to neuron to arrive at the medial temporal lobe and make their way to the hippocampus.

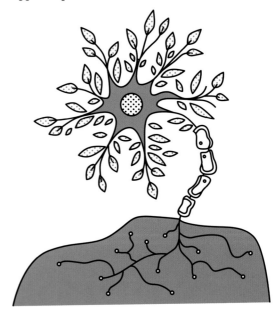

Zoom in on a single neuron in the path. Let's call him Fred. Fred receives incoming energy in the form of sodium ion inflows at several of its synaptic connections with many other upstream neurons. If the combined energy Fred receives is small, it could dissipate without Fred passing it along. However, if the energy builds to a high enough level, Fred will fire and send energy to his neighboring downstream neurons. Think of Fred retweeting your incoming brand message.

After firing, Fred may "reward" the incoming synapses by adding receptors at those synapses and turning on neighboring silent synapses by popping magnesium ion plugs out of their receptors. In simpler terms, think of Pop Rocks candy exploding a path through the brain. Makes "blowing your mind" rather relevant, right? Fred has now chosen to follow the group of neurons that are carrying your brand messages.

These changes in structure amplify Fred's response to the next waves of incoming energy from the same upstream neurons and result in long-term potentiation, a channel that stays open for hours or days waiting for new incoming energy. Think of it as a cattle gate, open and ready for more memories (cattle) to be herded inside. If none are received, the gate closes. Thus, brand experiences actually change brain chemistry, while silence leads to dormant neurons. Have you ever seen an old western ghost town? That's your brain on a lack of memorable experiences. Intriguing for academics to explore but sad for brand managers.

When incoming pulses continue over time, further changes will happen in the genetic expression at the neuron's nucleus that can trigger the formation of new synapses to add further responsiveness. As this long-term potentiation memory is consolidated through sleep or other means, something marvelous happens—you try to read an obnoxiously long term that means nothing to you, but a lot to the scientists studying memory. The term is cytoplasmic polyadenylation element binding protein, and we'll call it a binding protein, because binding is good and protein shakes are good for you. Because neuroscientists see neurons expressing this binding protein during the memory consolidation process and because this binding protein has the ability to sustain itself indefinitely, many believe it is a key ingredient in the formation of memories that could last a lifetime. So the memory is together until death do us part.

And you've done it. Your brand's moment has made it into deep long-term memory. Now you need to figure out how to retrieve those memories. If they are never accessed again, they might as well have never been planted. Your job is now to tend to the crop of memories that you have strategically planted in each person and throughout the world.

This is the most current science on the subject of memory encoding, yet we still don't know everything. But we do know that some memories are recorded in sequential space, and if a brand is encoded with a multisensory experience, the brand may be strong enough to become a part of the individual's life story. This interweaving of brands into our memories is obviously valuable to corporations, but also has value to the individual. If we're able to retrieve these memories, they offer all that a brand does the next time we're considering a transaction.

DID MR. FORBES DIE WITH ANY MEMORIES?

LONG-TERM MEMORIES RECALLED

"He who dies with the most toys wins," said Malcolm Forbes, a publisher and icon who certainly gathered enough toys to shout out "winner, winner, chicken dinner." But perhaps the Forbes quote needs two revisions: "The one who dies with the most memories wins," and, adding another layer, "the one who dies with the most retrievable memories wins." As we move from the gathering and storing of memories, we'll learn that all those Forbes motorcycles have no real utility value if you can't ride them or remember them. Retrieval is the skeleton key to the rusty cage of our minds, and we may not be able to find the key when we need it. And someone, perhaps from your community, or a brand handler or a brand owner, might hand you the key that unlocks the door to a purchase.

THOUGHT EXPERIMENT

WOULD READING EVERY WORD ON EVERY PACKAGE HELP US MAKE BETTER DECISIONS?

From here to eternity, in your memory at least, we'll explore how we recall memories. For example, we'll learn about how people with exceptional autobiographical memory (hyperthymesia)—like your high-school quarterback reliving the glory days—experience the world. We'll dig even deeper into what memory means for brands and people. Brands can only exist if they carry on in the memories of people. People meanwhile, can move from one brand to another; it all depends on the ability of a brand to remain in memory.

AN EXPONENTIAL UPPERCUT FROM DOLPH LUNDGREN

MEMORY HALF-LIFE

We have 100 years of data gathered by scientists to measure our ability to remember throughout our lifetimes. The data fits well to an exponential decay model, similar to the decay of nuclear radiation. The pesky isotope plutonium-239 is what you'd call a sticky customer with its half-life of 24,000 years, meaning half of its energy will have been spent in that time. To halve again will take another 24,000 years, and so on. Your brand should be so lucky to have customer retention rates like that. But beware, the plutonium-233 isotope has a half-life of twenty minutes.

Waloddi Weibull was a brilliant mathematician and at one time the fourth most famous person from Sweden, right behind Greta Garbo, Ingrid Bergman, and Dolph Lundgren. He discovered the Weibull distribution, which is based on an exponential function, and fits well with many customer retention patterns—for every 100 new customers, x percent will leave in the first year, y percent will leave in the second year, and so on until the curve of remaining customers flattens out to the most "sticky" customers. If a brand doesn't keep moving, evolving, and advancing forward, the declining memory curve of a Dolph Lundgren right hook will connect with your brand. Memory is a blunt and fickle thing. In order to remain relevant, brands need to keep adding value and engaging the senses.

The Weibull curve is often used by financial analysts to predict the value of future revenues from a company's existing customers. Since a brand relies on memories formed across space and time, and research indicates memories fade in time, it makes sense that we see a tendency toward exponential decay in customer relationships. Thank you Mr. Weibull for making a contribution we consider more memorable than those of your fellow Swedes, even Sly Stallone's nemesis, Dolph.

GET OFF YOUR ASTERISK AND SENSE IT*

FULL SENSORY RECALL

Have you noticed your body? Right now, while you're reading. Any posterior parts aching? Some say the mind can only hold as much as the rear end can endure. It's easy to get lost in thought when reading and lose connection to your body. As much as your mind and conscious self might not like the idea, your body is firmly in charge. Memories are formed through sensory experience and the resulting thoughts and feelings find a home in nerve cells.

Memory associations from multiple senses allow retrieval of the memory from multiple paths. Alternative paths of retrieval for implicit memories (a.k.a. habits) have been well studied. If the portion of the brain path that encodes a memory is damaged, another path can still lead to the memory. If both paths are damaged, the memory is a goner. This bundling of senses is a bountiful counter to the human memory half-life and certainly should push a brand toward designing more immersive experiences. Multi-sensory memories are stronger and stickier.

In this book, some of these words will stick, but most will fade away, influencing existing memories, beliefs, and desires along the way. To really remember a new idea, act! Make notes in the margins, have a coffee conversation with someone, share your insight on social media, write an action plan, then act. Moving your body leads to full sensory feedback that confirms or denies the utility of ideas, leading to stronger memories through more neural connections.

Action is critical for brands as well. Seeing a fifteen-second TV ad for a new Tesla is all well and fine, but it only deploys visual and auditory senses for a short bit of time. Compare that with going for a test drive, or better yet, compare it with the experience of owning a Tesla. Research shows that more sensory involvement leads to stronger memories, and more sensory involvement over time leads to subconscious habits. And enjoyable multisensory experiences over time lead to strong brands. So give your body a break. Get up, stretch out your arms, and give this some thought. Your senses and your asterisk will scream a thank-you.

THE OPTIMISTS WIN

POSITIVE EXPERIENCES = GOOD MEMORIES

Now for some good memory decay news. Research shows we tend to remember good experiences in full sensory detail, and the more we savor these memories, the longer the good times roll around in our heads. When brands provide pleasant experiences in full sensory detail such as smell, sight, and sound, people will not only have greater emotional connections to the brand, they will also remember the experiences longer. And the act of recall reinforces the memory for later recall.

To take this feel-good vibe one step further, studies show that people are irrationally optimistic about the future. Take diets as an example, or rock bands, or casinos, start-ups, or even marriage. People tend to believe they will enjoy the best outcomes even when they know the deck is stacked against them. Brands that provide an emotional appeal can find solace in this tendency. Within limits, the promise of a good time can even make an average branded experience feel special. People want to believe.

Optimism is wrapped up in our amygdala and hippocampus, two primitive neighbors

deep inside of our primitive "lizard brains." The amygdala is a power player, like the queen of a chess set, transmitting emotional orders all over the body. The hippocampus decides what is remembered and what falls to the cutting-room floor. Together these two organs direct our attention and memory. And this is one of the reasons we worked to inject a wink into our text now and again. More smiles, deeper memories.

Our friend the high-school quarterback who can't stop reliving the glory days could have a powerful hippocampus and a nostalgic amygdala. Oddly, the smell of locker rooms could be key to this phenomenon. The portion of the brain that processes smell is next door to the amygdala, which explains why so many strong emotions are brought up through scents. Likewise, scent can strengthen explicit autobiographical memories.

Our sense of smell is so strong that naming a positive odor, like roses, can bring the actual bouquet back to conscious experience for some people. The ability to see, hear, and smell something in their mind has been validated by seeing those sensory-processing portions of the brain light up in an fMRI or PET scan. Like our pal the quarterback, hyperthymesiacs, those rare individuals who can remember what they ate for lunch on the fourth of July in 2004, are known to have vivid sensory memory abilities as well. Both Mr. Quarterback and hyperthymesiacs use multisensory cues to create powerful memories that decay slowly.

For those of us without superautobiographical memory, a helpful memory-enhancing trick is to pay close attention to sensory details when we want to savor a particular experience later. For brand managers, it's clear that generating positive multisensory experiences will lead to longer-lasting memories and stronger brands. It's little wonder that quality is so often correlated with strong brands. Everyone wants to have a good time and then revel in the memories. Sometimes brands can help.

LIFE'S FOUR-ACT PLAY

PRIMACY, FREQUENCY, RECENCY, AND VELOCITY

The three-act play is a standard in the theater — and in life. Act One: we meet the characters. Act Two: the characters are involved in the drama of life. Act Three: the drama is temporarily resolved. Similarly, market researchers focus on memory with three key moments in the life of a brand: the first contact with people, the frequency of contact, and the last contact. And now we're adding one more act—Act Four, the change in the velocity of interactions.

Primacy is the bias toward remembering the input we received first versus middle or last. Frequency is the bias toward the input we received most often, and recency is the bias toward inputs we received most recently. These three terms are common in market research. Finally, we're adding velocity, the rate of change in frequency of contact with a brand. All four of these dimensions present an opportunity for brands to turn an ordinary experience into a memorable moment.

The primal "brand" in most of our lives is family. Family memories leave deep imprints in our brains. We spend more time with our families than other people in our most formative years. Nature even boosts neural connections during our early years. And it is likely our last significant emotional connection will be with family members. On top of this, our families gave us our personal brand names. Second to the importance of family are our friends and work colleagues. We more often than not like, respect, and trust our families and friends more than third parties. It is a challenge for brands to get inside these tight circles of community.

These are a few of many emotional and mental biases. There are hundreds of cognitive, social, and memory biases we rarely think about consciously. To compete with this dense network of human relationships, brands need to make sure that every signal is carefully orchestrated to leave a positive outcome. Since neurons that fire together wire together, it is critical that brands send the right signals.

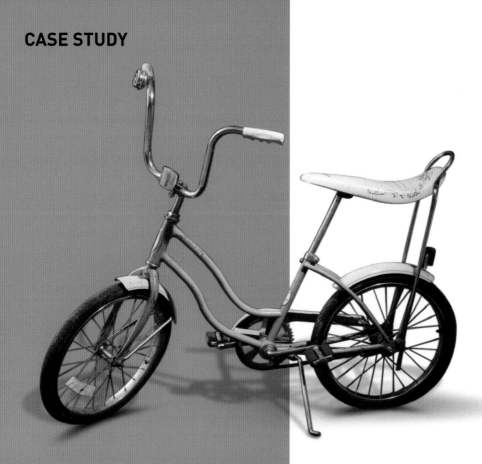

TWO WHEELS AND TIMING

THE SCHWINN BRAND

Think back on the years you learned to ride a bike. Perhaps you started on two wheels with training wheels wobbling to keep you upright. Remember the plastic rubbery feel of the handles? The smell of fresh spring air as you sped down the road at what had to be the fastest 5 mph in human history. Listening to the thwaping of your brother's Chicago Cubs baseball card in the front spokes. Then the screaming, wondering where it came from before you realized it was you after a yard sale kind of crash. The metallic taste of dirt as you spit it out along with enough blood to make Dad proud. Your parents came running, picked you up, checked for broken bones, only to find a bruised ego. The only thing that could have possibly made it better would have been Queen blaring "We Are the Champions" as the movie background sound.

This was a profound experience on so many levels for your brain. And not just because of the bouncing it took inside the helmet. It was an ideal age for your ability to recall the minute details from the event. The Schwinn brand formed a long-term memory through sensory input and the explosions happening inside your brain. Then you spent the next handful of summers perfecting your moves atop your two-wheeled freedom ride. More memories were embedded through friendships, adventures, alleys, and streets you explored. The Schwinn brand became a trusted companion, always capable of getting you there faster than on foot.

Take a second to recall. You can likely remember the rubber feel of the handlebar grips, the smell of chain grease and fresh-cut grass fields (also known as suburban yards). You had many memorable moments with this brand as a child, likely starting with the anniversary of your birth when it was presented to you in the drive. The first ride, likely the most compelling moment, as well as many other moments contributed to the bond you have with Schwinn. Now, shift twenty-five years to present time and the day you buy your child a bike has arrived. The visit to Target brings back all the memories as you spin the wheels, glide your hand over the seats, and feel the excitement building inside you. You take down almost every model, sometimes riding them down the aisle as the bike strains under your six-foot frame. After what could have been an hour-long selection process and a visit to the helmet section, you're wheeling a Schwinn into the check-out lane with a grin large enough to make the clerk question your sanity. You get home and your neighbor nods an affirming look, as his memories rush back and he will be making the same trip soon.

The real action takes place in the brain. Yet we also know that the brain creates an internal reality out of sensory input. A brand can affect time and space, and brands are affected by the spaces between ears, eyes, nose, fingers, and throat.

Go ahead; put this book down and go take your old Schwinn out of the garage and ride it one more time around the block. Your wife will understand. What better way to spend an hour of your Saturday morning than remembering what it felt like to achieve such transportation freedom at such a young age? Please remember to wear a helmet. That thing bobbing atop your spine is the reason you're able to have this memory. It would be sad and ironic to leave part of this important organ on the pavement.

REMEMBER WHAT YOU FORGOT—HUH?

CONCLUDING MEMORIES

IN SOME CIRCLES OF TRADITIONAL MARKETING, EDUCATING THE CUSTOMER IS CONSIDERED EXPENSIVE AND NOT WORTH THE INVESTMENT. WHAT ARE YOU TRYING TO DO WHEN YOU EDUCATE? HELP SOMEONE LEARN SOMETHING, EMBEDDING SOMETHING IN LONG-TERM MEMORY, PERHAPS? IN MANY WAYS MARKETING IS A COUSIN TO EDUCATION. MARKETING NEEDS TO SOLVE PROBLEMS OF DAILY LIFE WHILE KEEPING AN EYE ON THE BROADER CULTURE. AN EXPONENTIAL DECLINE IN MEMORIES IS ONE OF THE BIGGEST CHALLENGES MARKETERS FACE. IN THIS CHAPTER, WE LOOKED AT THE RUGGED AND CHALLENGING PATH TO MAKING A MEMORY.

(1) We understand as much about the human brain as we do the known universe. Yes, this is a small amount, but what we do know can be put to good use. Brain science cannot replace the art of branding, but it can direct it.

(2) Branding is sending signals to senses to create and accumulate long-term memories. Our brains have several independent pathways to process and store memories. These pathways can interact and associate several types of stored memories from the same experience.

(3) High sensory and/or emotional experiences can more easily create long-term memories. If we want to have someone recall an experience with a brand, the chances are better if more senses were involved in creating the memory.

(4) Memories decay. A sticky memory has a long half-life of decay. A sticky memory makes a sticky brand. A brand should aspire to have the half-life of radioactive waste.

(5) Continued and immersive multisensory experiences with a brand can add new memories and refresh old ones, leading to habits of buying a brand, creating more memories, and on and on it goes.

07

ENERGY + VALUE

STRAP ON YOUR JETPACK! THIS IS WHERE WE CONVERT MEM-
ORIES TO ENERGY TO BRAND VALUE. YOU'LL MOVE OUT OF
MEMORY TO THE PLACES WHERE VALUE IS CREATED FOR THE
INDIVIDUAL AND THE CORPORATION. WE'LL TAKE YOU TO THE
EDGE OF THE EMOTIONAL CHASM AND SHOW HOW WE CAN
GET SMARTER ABOUT THE MEASUREMENT OF MOMENTS.
YOU'LL BE GOING INTO MICRO-MOTIVATORS AND CUSTOMER
UTILITY AND BACK OUT TO MACROECONOMICS. ALL WITHIN
THE SAFETY OF THESE PAGES—YOUR JETPACK IS A METAPHOR.
TO SHARPEN THE CONTRAST OF THESE CONCEPTS,
WE EXPLORE A WORLD WITHOUT BRANDS AND A WORLD WITH
PERFECT KNOWLEDGE OF ALL BRANDS. THIS IS ALSO THE
PLACE WHERE YOU MIGHT WANT TO SHARE THIS BOOK WITH
THE CFO. SHE'LL BE IMPRESSED AND CURIOUS AT THE SAME
TIME, WHICH COULD BE A JETPACK FOR YOUR CAREER.

FIGURE 1.3: JACOB'S LADDER

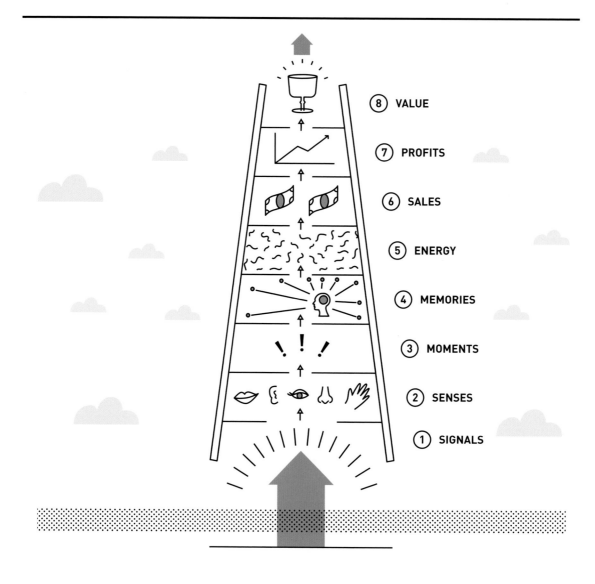

(8) VALUE

(7) PROFITS

(6) SALES

(5) ENERGY

(4) MEMORIES

(3) MOMENTS

(2) SENSES

(1) SIGNALS

THE MAGICAL ELIXIR

BRAND ENERGY AND VALUE

Brand energy is the mysterious element that gives brands value, and while we can define the contours of brand energy and use those concepts to help value a brand, we can't nail brand energy to a wall and measure it. Brand energy is like jelly, or perhaps mercury—it's a shape shifter that changes form depending on the facts and circumstances of each situation. One thing we know for sure is that brand energy resides in people, and specifically, inside of their brains' emotional charges. It always comes back to brain.

One of our contributions to the conversation about brand energy and value is Jacob's Ladder (Figure 1.3), the movement from signals, to senses, to moments, to memory, to energy, to sales, to profits, to value. We named this supermodel Jacob's Ladder after the climbing arc (think Frankenstein movies) that increases voltage and creates plasma, the fourth state of matter after solids, liquids, and gases. Plasma is a bit mysterious, like brand energy. Other common usages for Jacob's ladder include a stairway to heaven, an exercise equipment brand that never ends, and a horror film. You could make an argument that these alternative meanings make sense as well.

As we've explored this theory of brand energy, we acknowledge every situation is a unique case. That said, there are things we do know and can know about brand energy and its relation to brand value.

BLACKBERRIES GO BANANAS

THE SUMMIT BEYOND UNAIDED RECALL

Making memories is an essential process for building brands. This has not gone unnoticed by marketing theorists and practitioners. Unaided brand awareness is the gold standard for quantitative consumer research, used by brand managers the world over as a benchmark for success. However, strong memories by themselves don't guarantee a financially successful brand.

Ask people to name the first two brands they know in fresh fruit, or more specifically, bananas, and you'll likely get a large percentage recalling Chiquita and even a reasonable percentage who are able to crudely draw the logo of the woman with a fruit basket hat. Great, yet look into the recent history of the banana industry and you'll notice Miss Chiquita has had to hand over her glamorous hat to a bankruptcy court. The good news is that Miss Chiquita has a lesson to share: 100 percent unaided recall doesn't mean you have an impenetrable brand or business strategy. Now here is where that little voice in your head says, well, I liked her hat but she was in a commodity category where a banana is a banana is a banana. Let's look at another fruit, BlackBerry.

Ask people to name three mobile phone brands and they will likely name the one that broke through with an appropriate and indicative nickname, crackberry. Yet, this is also a brand that has lost its way due to a shift in the marketplace they could see, but couldn't culturally match. Certainly BlackBerry wasn't in a commodity marketplace, and likely held nearly a 100 percent

WHO CAN MEASURE BRAND ENERGY?

IF THERE WERE A GROUP OF PEOPLE WHO COULD FIGURE OUT HOW TO MEASURE BRAND ENERGY, IT WOULD BE A CONGRESS OF BEHAVIORAL ECONOMISTS, NEUROSCIENTISTS, MARKETERS, APPRAISERS, PSYCHOLOGISTS, AND PHILOSOPHERS. EACH WOULD LIKELY CLAIM THE AREA OF PRODUCT CHOICE DECISIONS AS THEIR DOMAIN, AND GETTING TO CONSENSUS WOULD BE ABOUT AS EASY AS TUNING YOUR BRAIN TO OPERATE LIKE A COMPUTER, DAY IN, DAY OUT. THAT IS ONE OF THE CHALLENGES OF MEASURING BRAND ENERGY. BRAND ENERGY LIVES IN OUR BRAINS, NO TWO BRAINS ARE ALIKE, AND ALL BRAINS CHANGE FROM MOMENT TO MOMENT. ADD TO THIS THE FACT THAT MANY BRAINS DISAGREE FROM MOMENT TO MOMENT.

unaided awareness, yet the company found its way onto a number of "when will they file bankruptcy?" lists in the financial media. So unaided awareness is not the gold standard, or brand standard, unless you're fine with settling for "fool's gold."

Chiquita and BlackBerry missed some key steps in the Jacob's Ladder model: Signals > Senses > Moments > Memories > Energy > Sales > Profits > Value. As you can see, awareness through moments and memories has a distance to travel before a brand adds value to its owner.

The juicy question is, Why did Chiquita and BlackBerry turn into overripe brands? By our analysis, Chiquita lost luster due to a 100-year history of virtual monopoly power that included environmental and worker exploitation and even funding paramilitary groups considered terrorist organizations, resulting in a $25 million lawsuit by the U.S. government. This is what is known as bad PR and negative brand energy.

BlackBerry's woes can be encapsulated in one phrase: iPhone disbelief. BlackBerry management believed the cellular networks couldn't handle the data required by the iPhone and, instead of innovating, made a bet on the iPhone's failure. Brands cannot avoid the negative effects of community anger over corporate misdeeds, nor can brands easily overcome missing an innovation cycle as large as the iPhone. The utility the brand delivers must advance at the pace of the category cycle of innovation or fail. Competitors are also building brand memories. A person's decision of whether to buy your product at any point in time depends upon his perception of expected utility, risk, price, and the cost of his time to make the decision. Sometimes competing offers just look better, especially when energy from the person's community is giving the competitor velocity. Is that an iPhone in your pocket?

One of our authors used to create advertising campaigns for a circuit board company that was known for its quality. Unfortunately, in a drive for profit, cost cutting led to a decline in that quality, and customers started defecting. Their customers experienced surprises when actual utility came up short of their expected utility, injecting negative energy. This caused the customers to reassess the risk and expected utility in their next purchase decisions. The panicked client called a meeting to see if advertising could solve the problem. It seems everyone wants to believe in magic.

THE LOGIC OF EMOTION

LOVE, HATE, AND THE APATHETIC

The fight between the heart and the head has probably been going on since cave dwellers turned grunts, dances, and melodies into words. The European Enlightenment sought to create a world dominated by logic once and for all, but so far, if you look around, it has not worked out very well. Love and hate seem to drive more of human behavior than we'd like to admit, and smart designers use the polarities of love and hate to do research that surfaces hidden desires.

The mere thought of considering love and hate is likely to create apoplectic rage in the modern corporation—an imaginary child of the Enlightenment era. Delaware corporate legal charters are designed to "manage" a "process" toward a predictable outcome, with emotional extremes removed. If that does not happen, Wall Street lawyers and the HR police are waiting to punish offenders. Marketers and innovators are often the odd ones in corporate environments, which may partially explain the short tenure of chief marketing officers in this turbulent digital age.

Yet if you search for love or hate, you'll find passion. In many cases you'll find passion that is misinformed, misguided, and missing a few bricks in the chimney, but emotions do not lie. In cultures that are afraid to offend, "I'm offended" bumper stickers can become the norm. The result is brands that are acceptable to all and interesting to none, leading to apathy.

Madison Avenue in the 1960s had an intuitive grasp of the power of emotion. Even back in the forties advertising copywriters would keep secret lists of compelling desires in their top desk drawer that recorded basic desires like food, sex, nurturing the young, and social approval. A common slogan in the ad world is "people decide on emotion and justify with facts." Mass advertising has seen happier days, but this insight still holds water.

Recently, brainy academics have been taking a close look at human passions, and indicators point to the heart being a constant companion to the head. Nobel Prize–winning economist Daniel

THE EFFECTS OF EFFECTS

WHILE IT IS EASY TO PICK ON THE HIERARCHY OF EFFECTS MODEL, THE ADVANCEMENT OF THE THINKING TO MODERN CONSTRUCTS IS DONE WELL BY BAMBANG SUKMA WIJAYA IN "THE DEVELOPMENT OF A HIERARCHY OF EFFECTS MODEL IN ADVERTISING." THE ADDITIONS OF SOME MODERN MEDIA TERMS SUCH AS SEARCH, LIKE/DISLIKE, SHARE, AND LOVE/ HATE GIVE US A MODERN SPIN ON A CENTURY-OLD STRUCTURE. THE LAST BIG MOVEMENT IN THE HIERARCHY OF EFFECTS MODEL CAME WITH THE ADDITION OF A LOYALTY CONSTRUCT. WE SEE LOYALTY MEASURED TODAY IN THE FORM OF A NET PROMOTER SCORE, OR "WOULD YOU RECOMMEND THIS TO A FRIEND?" BRAND ENERGY IS SEVERELY AFFECTED BY NEGATIVE PUBLICITY AND NEGATIVE SURPRISES. A SURPRISINGLY POSITIVE EXPERIENCE CAN GIVE BRAND ENERGY A BOOST AND TRIGGER THE SPREAD OF ENERGY TO THE PERSON'S COMMUNITY. WE'VE ALREADY TALKED ABOUT HOW STRONG EMOTIONS MAKE STRONG MEMORIES. EMOTIONS ALSO GENERATE ENERGY.

THOUGHT EXPERIMENT

WHEN WOULD THE BRAND OF POWER COMPANY YOU BUY
ELECTRICITY FROM MATTER MORE THAN THE CAR YOU DRIVE?

Kahneman discovered that people do not always make rational economic decisions. Neuroscientists have discovered that our emotionally active amygdala has an oversized voice in our behavior, and there is no centralized logical governor in our brains. What is certain is that math, science, and logic do not govern our daily behaviors. Though if we had to pick a centralized governor, it would likely be an Italian actress, unafraid to throw her arms up in a rage at the drop of an unfashionable handbag. When grocery stores stock around 40,000 brands on shelves and Amazon contains more than 150,000,000 brands and products, emotion is actually a logical way to decide from which store to buy. In a world of abundant choice, needs become wants. Logically quantifying all the variables would surely make even the largest computer freeze. As we age and gain much-needed experience, we rely more on our gut and may even say in a meeting, "Those numbers don't feel right." We may believe we're thinking, but whether we know it or not, we're feeling, and then thinking.

THUMBS UP OR MIDDLE FINGER UP

POSITIVE, NEUTRAL, OR NEGATIVE MOMENTS

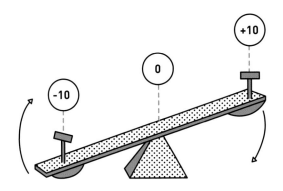

Moments can form a spectrum of negative, to neutral, to positive memories. Each impression leaves a lasting impression in the brain. This shouldn't be considered a binary system, but rather a range, from -10 to 0 to +10 as an example.

And research shows that negative effects have double the impact of positive effects. Only counting likes can work in Facebook, but not in the commercial world. Dislikes offer a much-needed contrast.

There are classic rubrics, like news of a bad experience reaches twice as many eyes and ears as praise for the positive experience. And 80 percent of companies say they deliver "superior" customer service, yet 8 percent of customers think these same companies actually do. Or, it takes twelve positive experiences to make up for one unresolved negative one. These are all motivation for change. They all point to the importance of positive moments. This is important, because consistent quality is highly correlated with strong brands.

Think of it through the lens of physics. In order to have matter in the universe we also have antimatter. Negative moments neutralize positive and balance the experience. Unlike trophies for just showing up, not every brand can win. And this is as good a place as any to bust out the Louisville Slugger on the concept of delighting every customer. The economic cost of delighting every customer is unachievable.

For that matter, many customers haven't paid enough to buy delight. Put this aside. It is a pie crust promise to believe you can achieve 100 percent delight, because if you don't have the "less than delighted," contrast can't be achieved. Plus don't we learn the most from the most challenging (interpret as less than delighted) customers?

People don't have a 1–5 ranked experience; they have a negative or positive experience. The challenge with the 1–5 feel-good ranking is that even a 1 makes a positive contribution to the outcome, when in fact a 1 to a customer is a negative experience and likely wipes out any recent positive experience and drops the energy meter to zero. This built-in mathematical bias has led us to believe average ratings are okay, when in fact they could be signaling a very negative situation.

Brand owners can learn more from those who have the polarizing experiences (-10 or +10). Not all moments make a contribution to brand value—some subtract.

IF WE'RE NOT MOVING, WE'RE DYING

THE ORIGIN OF MOTIVATION

Sadly, we all die someday. This simple fact guides much of our motivation when we make decisions that translate energy into sales. When speaking of what moves us to action in favor of a brand, we need to cover two areas of study: motivation and persuasion. Motivation comes from inside the cellular walls of our brains, influenced by the world around us. Persuasion gives us some of the shortcuts we are prone to as human beings. Persuasion is the yeast, while motivation is the flour, eggs, water, and other important ingredients for a handcrafted loaf of bread.

Motivation is evolutionary. The fact that we are hardwired to weigh downside risk about twice as much as upside gain makes sense when you think about it. Imagine the African savanna thousands of years ago. A lone hunter sees rustling in the grass. It could be predator or prey. He's trying to impress the girl in the village with his hunting prowess, and he needs to raise his status with her family, so he lunges into the grass with a spear, only to be met by a lion. So ends his line of DNA. No wonder the human race is so twitchy.

We have sharp wits, loud voices, but no fur, fangs, or claws. Yet working with other humans, we invented weapons that wiped out mammoths and saber-toothed tigers. And through language and opposable thumbs we created technology that reshaped the earth in ways that are clearly visible from outer space. Geologists call ours the Anthropocene age. Geologists see the really long view of history.

Fear aside, we're motivated to be safe, loved, and respected. We certainly have biological needs for shelter, clothing, food, and water, but none of these creature comforts are stable without the goodwill of others. Family, friends, and tribal relationships are ideally a safe haven and bulwarks against fear. Brands are safe havens, too. Arizona State University professor Robert Cialdini has isolated these six factors of persuasion that make a lot of intuitive sense: fair relationships, consistent qualities, social proof from others, the authority of the source, likability, and scarcity.

Our brains are wired to be social. Babies immediately stare into the eyes of their mom. Mirroring neurons help us estimate what others are feeling and thinking. Language and art evolved entirely for community life. And our most powerful memories are social. Some creatures are born to be solitary, but people are tribal by nature.

Today in Western societies, we've urbanized to create dense human jungles, places where people and relationships are more transient and social relationships can change fortunes quickly. Brands become proxies for real relationships in this new world, and they become social signals that urban Westerners use to find friends and mates. An iPhone is much more than a phone; it's a virtual friend and a status symbol.

There are two important types of motivation: intrinsic and extrinsic. Intrinsic motivation comes from within the person with less concern for the external reward. An example is someone who is curious about a subject, object, person, or place because, logical or not, she has an internal drive to move in that direction. Extrinsic motivation comes from outside forces compelling someone to move toward a socially validated reward. Dig deep into the psychology of motivation and you'll find the "how to raise your kids" debate with either an extrinsic reward system or the intrinsic code that motivates your child to clean her room.

Applied to brands, the intrinsically motivated—specific to your category—are much easier to motivate in your direction because they are already fans of your category or hopefully of your brand. Audiences that require extrinsic motivation are going to need a cattle prod to the "upper thigh" region, social pressure from the intrinsic crowd, or something financial to motivate them in your direction. An easy way to understand extrinsic versus intrinsic motivation is to consider a baseball player who plays for his own internal reward, for the sake of how it pleases him to do so. This is in contrast with the baseball player who may have started with intrinsic motivations, but eventually plays for the money and fame.

Let's just look at audience pools that have an intrinsic motivation in your direction. You might already have a name for them: heavy users, fanatical fans, loyalists. They are motivated in your direction due to internal forces within them and you play an important role in their lives. They don't need to be rewarded, and in fact, studies have shown that rewarding this audience with fake currency, financial rewards, or other extrinsic rewards is counterproductive. Start paying them to show up and the offers are interpreted as fake, disingenuous, or, worse, offensive. If you see audiences as consumers and group them together in traditional demographic and psychographic profiles, this can eat at the foundation of a trusted relationship with some of your most important audiences.

THE MICRO-MOTIVATORS

THE ECONOMICS OF OUR BRAND CHOICES

We can't finish our discussion on motivation without giving the microeconomists some air time. Brands provide five wonderful economic benefits:

- BRANDS ARE SHORTCUTS AND THEREFORE REDUCE TIME AND HASSLE FOR SEARCH.

- BRANDS DECREASE THE CHANCE OF A BAD PURCHASE BY OFFERING A CONSISTENT CHOICE.

- BRANDS REDUCE PRICE TO THE INDIVIDUAL BY ACHIEVING SCALE ECONOMIES.

- WE ENJOY THE SOCIAL UTILITY BRANDS PROVIDE US IN OUR COMMUNITY.

- BRANDS PROVIDE PEOPLE WITH A PERSONAL EXPRESSIVE UTILITY.

Buying anything has many nuances involved that are yet to be understood. From a rational economic perspective, it generally makes sense to save and not spend, yet we are always tempted to spend. There are as many social theories about why we spend as there are ways to take a selfie. Brands have turbocharged the economy and the economy has rewarded brands.

Products and services themselves provide utility value that is directly tied to motivation. You need to get across town and one form of transportation will get you there faster but may cost you more. The economics of persuasion come down to choices, but we often get stuck in the sidewalk bubblegum of cultural norms. Commuting to work on a bike may take fifteen minutes longer, but you'd be able to cancel your gym membership. These rational "economic" reasons still face the social awkwardness of showing up sweaty at work. Raw economics meets social reality every day.

The utility value brands provide offers us reasons to buy and persuades using the logical better choice. Even when we put these decisions through a logical filter, they can never be removed from the emotional machine that drives us.

THOUGHT EXPERIMENT

WHAT WOULD A DAY IN A WORLD WITHOUT BRANDS BE LIKE?

Rather than telling us how rational beings should decide, the field of behavioral economics looks at how actual humans make decisions and then tries to explain them. Turns out, we're not very logical.

Irrational behavior is in the uneducated eye of the beholder. We build a life-sized sand castle to support decisions we can't explain rationally. This sand castle is built from small grains of less-understood behaviors. When we study these under a microscope to see the why, we might discover these are, in some way, rational behaviors, after all. We just didn't understand the problem people were solving in the first place. Hence, the behavioral economists hope to rationalize persuasion and motivation, explaining art with science.

ADAM SMITH AND KARL MARX WALK INTO A BAR

CUSTOMER UTILITY

The great-great-grandfather of economics, Adam Smith, set a foundation for free market economics. Then Karl Marx gave us the theory of socialism, with capitalism breaking down to form a classless system. Wouldn't you want to see Adam Smith meet Karl Marx in a bar just to see if a brawl broke out? Well, today our branded world would certainly put Karl Marx at a disadvantage, as Adam Smith could break an empty bottle of Scotch whiskey over Karl's head. The invisible hand of the market won by delivering superior customer utility.

One thing Adam and Karl would not have argued about is the added value of brands, for brands were mere infants 200 years ago, and giants today. Lack of competition and innovation are deficits in the communist system, but, to its credit, communism did not burden people with choice. In fact, there were basically no choices, and often few goods, period. The free market system is competitive, innovative, and filled with choice, which has its own problems. Brands help people navigate crowded commercial landscapes to make wise and safe choices that optimize

customer utility. Through these choices, brands gain scale and become efficient, which reduces cost and price while increasing profit. Brands have an invisible hand to guide them toward this hat trick.

To really understand the power of brands in our economy and society, imagine a world without brands. No brand names, logos, or colorful packages, no advertising—just generic descriptions of ingredients and product benefits. Shopping would be a major ordeal because you'd have to assess the safety and value of every product you come across. No goods would have an advantage or be recognizable, no manufacturer would have an incentive to maintain quality or innovate, and lack of scale would mean higher costs and prices. This fictional world would operate like an ancient open-air marketplace, or like cold war–era communist China and Russia, with poorly stocked shelves featuring subpar products. Brands are an economic engine of intangible assets used in the exchange of goods and services (let's collectively refer to them as offerings). Fundamentally, you can break down any financial exchange into three parts: (1) the cost to create the offering; (2) the profit taken by the seller between the cost and the price; and (3) the value the buyer gets beyond the price paid. Few transactions beyond the lemonade stand have this level of simplicity.

Owners of brands with a critical mass of followers can harness the power of efficient scale to reduce the manufacturing cost and increase profits, while also reducing the price to the customer. It's kind of magical when you think about it. Everybody seems to win.

But then there is the challenge of choosing the right brand. With more than 3 million brands in the world, we have a lot of choices. Just take a walk down the aisle of a grocery store to pick out a bottle of shampoo or deodorant. Choice alone becomes stressful, and even more stressful when you factor in the status anxiety of what a brand may say about you.

Some people are naturally risk averse and unwilling to experiment if they find a satisfactory product, even though there may be a product out

TAKING LEAPS OF MOVIE MAGIC

NETFLIX WAS FOUNDED WHEN THE CREDITS WERE JUST STARTING TO SCROLL ON THE BRICK-AND-MORTAR DELIVERY OF MOVIE RENTALS. THE NETFLIX MODEL OF DELIVERING A DVD TO YOUR DOOR AND ALLOWING YOU TO SET UP A QUEUE OF THE MOVIES YOU'D GET DELIVERED WAS ADOPTED FASTER THAN THE EXISTING COMPETITIVE PLAYERS WERE WILLING TO ADMIT TO THEMSELVES OR THEIR SHAREHOLDERS. INSTEAD OF SITTING ON THIS ACCOMPLISHMENT, NETFLIX LEAPT FORWARD TO STREAMING CONTENT FOR A SIMILAR MONTHLY SUBSCRIPTION. AGAIN, NOT SITTING BACK ON THEIR LAURELS, NETFLIX MADE A LEAP INTO ORIGINAL CONTENT. IF YOU OWNED THE STOCK, YOU NOTICED. IN JUST OVER A DECADE, THE BRAND OF NETFLIX MOVED FROM A CONTENT DISTRIBUTION BRAND TO A VERTICALLY INTEGRATED CONTENT CREATION AND DISTRIBUTION BRAND WITH AN INTERNATIONAL AUDIENCE. LIKE A PERSON, IF YOU'RE NOT MOVING, YOU'RE LIKELY DEAD.

there better suited. Other people are more open to taking risks and will be the first adopters. They may get a utility boost from the social joy and status from showing their friends a unique find.

The status of brand choice combined with what a brand may say about you has become more important with the triumph of free market capitalism. Given the dynamic nature of constantly changing capitalist economies, people use brands now to position themselves in society, establish a sense of self, and attach to something constant. In a world of choice, wants become needs, and brands become merit badges. Capitalism did not solve the issue of social class, although many brands are certainly heading in that direction. So let's score a counterpunch from Karl Marx.

PUTTING A BOUNTY ON THE HEAD OF A BRAND

WHAT IS A BRAND WORTH?

Suppose your CFO wants to know why you should invest in branding. Or let's say you need to sell a brand. Maybe someone has been trading under your brand name and you are going to sue them for damages. Or perhaps you want to license a brand name to use on products you produce. In all of these cases, you need to establish the value of a brand. This is difficult, because technically a brand is simply a government license, a piece of paper. Good thing is, there are ways and means.

One way is for a broker to set up an auction and let the market answer the question of your brand's value. Management might cite internal metrics or their own gut instinct gleaned from watching their stock price react to brand-related news to further articulate brand value. An advertising agency might offer to supply a value from a proprietary black-box model. You could also hire an appraiser to use a range of techniques, including looking for evidence of similar brands being licensed or sold, quantifying management's expected share of product profits contributed by the brand, and, possibly, finding the expected costs to re-create existing brand value.

A brand value appraiser would also ask: "As of when? To whom? Under what conditions? Using what standard? Along with what other assets?" The appraiser would also likely value the components of what we mean by a "brand," such as trademarks, trade names, customer relationships, customer lists and other customer data, product designs, artwork, domain names, and agreements pledging or securing rights related to the brand. Brand value appraiser questions are, by necessity, exhaustive.

Most answers to, "How do you value a brand?" will involve finding evidence of third-party exchanges for similar assets, as well as the value of future cash flows generated by the brand. This assumes the expected financial benefits to those who obtain rights to the brand are in line with the prices and rates paid between third parties for those rights. Yes, it is complicated.

Our work has brought us to a different question that, once answered, can deepen everyone's insight into how a particular brand should be valued. We ask the question, "Why does a brand have value?" Further, "Whose value are we valuing? Value to the owner or value to customer, or both?"

Our models around time and space provide a new framework to explore new brand valuation methods in the emerging world of massive data. The sources of brand value are becoming clearer every day and will be explored in depth in the following chapter.

BUY THE COW OR GET THE MILK FOR 23 PERCENT LESS?

THE COST TO DEVALUE A BRAND

Another way to understand the value of a brand is to undercut its price. In a commodity scenario, what unit of price reduction would break up a brand relationship? Let's compare a couple of scenarios in which parity happens and a change in behavior occurs.

For example, let's say Spirit Airlines is betting a $100 decrease in a round-trip ticket to Los

Angeles will buy you off your preferred option of Delta Air Lines. And if you've interacted with the world of airline ticket pricing specialists, you know these are some of the most sophisticated mathematical minds in marketing (perhaps only second to actuaries at insurance brands). Pricing in the world of airlines is a scientific priority and an artistic masterpiece when it works. So in this instance, you could argue Delta commands a 31 percent price premium (which is the same thing as saying Spirit is offering a 24 percent price discount off of Delta's price), although all the silly airline games cloud the issue.

Compare this with the simple cost of gas for your vehicle. What price per gallon of gas would you guess might change consumer behavior? How about an increase from $1.90 (Nov 2015 prices) to $5.30 per gallon, which is where Gallop predicted the price needs to be to change behaviors. If that were the case, you'd pay an additional $3.40 per gallon, or $51.00 per visit to the pump on a 15-gallon tank. At 34 percent more cost, some people will find a way to buy less gas. In the flight situation, Spirit is betting that a 24 percent discount will change your behavior.

Now let's compare the behavioral changes. For the airlines, it starts with a move of the mouse to click on a better price—then enduring lowered expectations traveling with a discounted option and all the behaviors included. For some travelers, it might feel like the difference between going to a movie or watching Netflix on the couch. For the gallon of gasoline at the pump, it could mean small changes in lifestyle (driving less, walking more, a flying instead of driving vacation), or it could mean dramatic changes (buying an electric car, taking the bus, or exposing your bum to a bike seat). While these behavioral changes can be drawn back to the price per barrel of crude, they are vastly different. These decisions, like all decisions, are emotional. Some would say this is a comparison between apples and oranges. We would say it's closer to comparing the Hubble telescope to eyeglasses. There are vast economic structures between these two scenarios, yet they both focus our attention on the price to change behaviors.

THOUGHT EXPERIMENT

WITH DIGITAL PRICING ON GROCERY SHELVES, HOW WOULD AIRLINE PRICING METHODS IMPACT BEHAVIORS?

THE WILD AND WOOLLY WORLD OF BRAND VALUE

A WORLD WITHOUT BRANDS

A marketing professional might answer the question "How do you value a brand?" by using surveys, market share, and other metrics to measure what marketers call brand equity—a theoretical concept indirectly linked to financial value. Legal scholars explore this question to weigh the benefits of intellectual property protection against antitrust issues. Economists approach this from a macroeconomic, industrial organization perspective, assuming worlds with producers maximizing profits and customers maximizing utility.

Let's take a look at this, but first go back for a moment to the world without brands. The former Soviet Union removed all brands and belief in brands. Mother Russia was the only brand in which to believe and know. If any country could achieve this, it would be a strong state-controlled environment in which the price of any given service or item would be its cost after the state took its cut. Everything was price controlled and the names (what we would call brand names) would be owned by the state. The name wouldn't matter because everything would be priced the same. If there were a shortage of one item, we would be required to replace it with another (toilet paper for paper towels or running shoes for slippers).

There was no motivation to innovate, and since factory managers could be shot if they missed quotas, they simply promised small amounts of goods while requesting larger amounts of vodka. This describes the situation before the Berlin Wall fell. Soon after the fall, great demand for brands opened up as Russian citizens made visits to the United States, coming back with Levi's and Gucci.

What do we learn from an exercise such as this? Without brands, people will buy products and customer utility exists. Life does go on, but not with the same deliciousness as a life with brands. Without free markets and brands,

innovation is nonexistent and the price of poor-quality goods is high. Brands are part of our lives and there's no way around it. It also appears that the desire for status is woven into our DNA. And if brands and people occupy the same space and time, economic value is created. This value we have yet to precisely define.

People want to purchase and consume products and services within the constraints of income, savings, or available credit. Producers sell at prices that are designed to maximize profits, given cost constraints. People pay attention to competing producers' offerings and prices. As time moves on, producers play a "game" to adjust their prices in response to competitors' prices to try to increase profits. If competing products and services are identical and there are no economies of scale, then brands will not matter. Without differentiation, brands don't really exist, and without brands and intellectual property, innovation withers.

This is the other path to our thought experiment of an unbranded world: a world with no innovation or scalable price advantage. Someone said, "Everything that can be invented, has been invented"—or maybe not. Though this quotation is commonly attributed to either Charles Holland Duell or Henry Ellsworth, ironically, both past U.S. Patent Office commissioners, it turns out that it is unlikely either of them actually said it. Nevertheless, the world this orphan quote depicts is a world in which brands can't survive. Without new innovations or producer value added to offerings, brands can't exist. Yes, the names and even trademarks exist, but because no new utility is added by producers. People only have price to make decisions.

These two theoretical paths to an unbranded world offer contrasting lessons: (1) Humans need brands nearly as much as we need fellow humans. (2) If brands don't provide added value to customers, those brands will disappear. (3) Without brands, there is no motivation to innovate or achieve scaled economic advantages.

Fortunately, we don't live in a future designed by Karl Marx or one in which we've hit our maximum invention potential.

NO MATTER WHAT SHE SAYS, SIZE DOESN'T MATTER

FROM MASS TO MICRO MARKETING

Because national brands have historically been built by "big advertising" budgets, there's a commonly held belief inside many organizations that the cost of building a national brand is high and out of reach to many corporations. This is changing and keeps changing. More brands are built with less or no advertising at all by, for example, designing a compelling product and leveraging social networks, news media, and the Internet to spread the word.

In short, brands are built one person at a time. Same as relationships. Value is offered by an organization. A human being obtains value. Upon this foundational exchange, a brand is built. This means that no matter how many customers you have, a brand exists. It also means that if you can spend less to form brand relationships, you likely have a stronger brand offering. Take it from a geek, Robert Stephens, founder of Geek Squad, who said it best: "Advertising is the tax you pay for being unremarkable." What does this really mean? There are two implications. First, a brand owner with imagination has greater odds than a brand owner with too much budget to spend. Second, geeks will eventually rule the world.

The economic value a brand provides to the corporation and the human being starts with one transaction. The importance of this thought needs to be considered with deliberation. Brands add social welfare one transaction at a time by matching customers to the products that suit them best. This increases total customer utility. Owners capture some of this added utility through increased prices and/or reduced costs and, in turn, increase producer profits. Many brand owners look at established brands as having more budget, and therefore a brand advantage, but this is not always the case. Sometimes they're just larger.

WOULD YOU LIKE A RIDE? PRESS THIS BUTTON

AN UBER EXPERIENCE

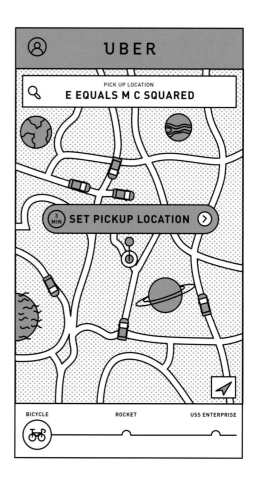

Consider the economics of auto transportation in large cities. The model hasn't changed for over fifty years. You step to the curb and attempt to get the attention of a passing cabbie. By all definitions, the marketplace had reached optimal efficiency, from the government and cabbie perspective. Yet there were cracks in the system. If you were new to a city, you were likely to be anxious about how you should tip and whether the cabbie was taking you the long way around. And if you've ever been to a large conference, exiting the airport and seeing the 100-plus-person line for cabs is rather demoralizing. The economic system was not optimized for the human being or to handle high-traffic periods.

During an evening on the town in Paris, legend has it, a group of wealthy Americans decided to rent town cars because they couldn't find cabs. That's how the idea of Uber was born.

If you haven't had the Uber experience, here are some essential moments contributing to brand value for this now estimated $40 billion venture. Just download the app and a map with little black car icons moving around slowly, kind of like a Nintendo game, will pop up. With the tap of your right thumb you "Request Uber" and a car immediately turns your way. Uber has just connected the physical and digital worlds. So you put your destination in, the Uber driver shows up, you get in, and he heads to your destination. He is like any other driver, yet somehow cleaner, less baked in smoke, and certainly cheery. Since Uber has your credit card on file, when you reach your destination, you simply get out of the car. This needs emphasis: You don't hassle with a credit card, a cash-only deal, or signing the smallest piece of paper ever. You just get out and go on with your life. Done.

Behind the scenes, the economic engines fighting the Uber expansion like a tractor pull include the unions and state governments. Your fee for travel in Uber doesn't include taxes, union dues, or a variety of other costs, which have piled up inside the cabbie system over the past half-century. You have just gained new utility value. Uber obtained brand value and the growth of new drivers using their cars while they're out anyway has gained economic value as well. This is what the horse-betting people call the trifecta of economic value obtained.

It all comes back to two highly compelling moments. The moment you requested an Uber and the moment you exited the car with a mere thank-you. The first moment was like a video game and put the control back in your hands (specifically your right thumb). The second moment was an absence of cultural anxieties you maybe didn't even realize were there. The absence is a moment of joy. If you've done the Uber thing, you know what it feels like.

DECISIONS, DECISIONS

UBER UNDER

As this book was being written, Nobel economist John Nash Jr., the inspiration for the movie *A Beautiful Mind*, died in a New Jersey taxi accident. With all the messaging being pushed by unions and government questioning the safety of an Uber ride, this beautiful mind and his wife died due to a taxi driver. We loved John Nash and all he accomplished for the world of economics and mathematics.

John introduced the Nash equilibrium: the idea that producers (brand owners) make decisions by considering their competitors' own decision-making process.

Consider what Delta Air Lines does when you click your mouse to purchase a flight. They might say, "Aha! Your utility of our brand experience is worth at least $100 premium over Spirit. What if we extract more value from you by raising it to a $150?" Secretly you would surrender your remaining customer surplus and still purchase from Delta, because the intangibles are worth it. Now wait, Delta might pause and wonder if Spirit would see you haven't taken their bait and drop their price by another $40. If Delta raises and Spirit drops, you will be looking at a $190 price difference. Those intangibles just became tangible in the form of 190 smackaroos. Move your mouse

THOUGHT EXPERIMENT

HOW WILL DRIVERLESS CARS CHANGE OUR LOVE AFFAIR WITH AUTOMOBILE BRANDS? AND WHO WOULD BUY A FERRARI VERSION OF A DRIVERLESS CAR?

to click the Spirit ride, but not so fast. Delta accurately predicts Spirit's response and instead holds pat. Delta gets the click. That is Nash equilibrium. Brand owners' lives would be easy if they only had to worry about price. Unfortunately, they face other headwinds. They are working with imperfect information, looking through a glass of murky water trying to guess what would delight you or if you're an odd duck not worth courting. They also have to decide what and where to invest in brand-building activities—mass-media advertising, public relations, social media, direct-to-consumer touches, experience design, digital, social media, and the list of mediums is growing. If you think you're challenged by choices, consider how many considerations the brand owner has to reach you. And then there is natural randomness to consider. It comes down to a simple question for brand owners: How do we design a moment to capture our audience's full attention and plant a positive memory?

YOUR DANCE WITH BRAND OWNERS?

MICRO, MACRO, AND BACK TO MICRO

Whether you realized it, you have just completed the first-semester course in microeconomics. Customers and Producers (Persons and Owners) are continuously doing a dance: theorizing, making decisions, seeing outcomes, changing choices, making more decisions, and so on. With the growth of big data, adding up all household-level decisions in microeconomics gives you macroeconomics. It's a twofer.

The promise of micro to macro and back to micro is a modeling of the "irrationality" in our personal choices exposed during the study of behavioral economics. It can explain purchases of toilet paper, market meltdowns, and, with good fortune, Care Bears.

SPACE FOOD? THAT'S CRAZY

PLUM ORGANICS

Neil Grimmer cofounded Plum Organics and grew it to nearly $41 million in sales within six years before selling to Campbell's. He states his inspiration was better food for his own children. But Neil and his team didn't just invent a new form of healthier, organic, or better-formulated baby food. They redesigned the consumption process for babies, kids, and adults. They designed a pouch with an easy-to-open, but hard-to-tamper-with, cap.

Neil happens to have a background in product design, so his affection for the human side of a business is deeply embedded. In a previous life he designed a "hug" machine, which was essentially a vest someone could wear. Similar to getting a "like" on Facebook, you could alternatively send someone a virtual hug. So Neil isn't a typical founder of a baby food venture, but then again, who really is.

NEIL GRIMMER GAVE BIRTH TO THE PLUM ORGANICS BRAND IN THE
BABY FOOD AISLE. THE ODD IMAGE IN YOUR HEAD WAS INTENTIONAL.
THE CHALLENGE OF DESIGNING A MOMENT SHOULD NEVER BE CONSIDERED
EASY, FAST, OR CHEAP (THOUGH SOMETIMES YOU CAN ACHIEVE TWO OF
THREE). IT TAKES A LOT MORE THAN SPREADSHEETS AND PRESENTATION
DECKS TO MAKE A MEMORY FOR A MOM AND HER HUNGRY INFANT.

In telling the story of starting his food venture, Neil describes a pace of product development closer to the software world: from toner on paper to the store in three months. While this sounds unrealistic if you're looking out the large glass windows of a corner office in the largest baby food corporation in the world, it is an entrepreneurial pace. What makes this story relevant to our conversation is Neil's observation of the moment in time and Plum Organics' most memorable moment.

The first opportunity to drop into retail came from Babies "R" Us, and Neil made himself present to do what we affectionately call "retail stalking." He observed moms shopping with their children. The first mom picked up the Plum pouch, said out loud to herself, "Okay, space food," and then promptly set it back in the display. Neil describes the panic that swept through him like a tropical fever. Then, just a few minutes later, another mom picked up the unusual package and said to herself loud enough for Neil to hear, "Well, that'll work." She promptly opened the package and handed it to her child, who started to draw food from the straw-like opening. Infant fed, she strolled on down the aisle to her next task. Neil's panic fell away as quickly as it had arrived and Plum Organics was off and running toward a bright new sunrise. He witnessed a monumental moment in the history of his young brand and a designed moment that he saw repeated many times in the future.

Let's look back and filter this story through the concepts presented in this chapter. The mom who engaged with the product certainly had no memory of the brand, but likely had constructs from her childhood that helped her make the leap. Depending on her age, the mobility of food may have taken the form of Popsicles or frozen push-ups. She had only the package to persuade her, but the perceived risk was likely small at a price point of $1.39 for the blueberry, pear, and purple carrot individual pouch.

The brand handler Babies "R" Us delivered the trust of a retailer with her interests in mind. She was motivated to keep her toddler fed and occupied during the thirty-minute task of finding a variety of other predetermined shopping items. The package design sent signals of quality fruits and vegetables in an easy-to-open and handle pouch. The word *organic* likely provided a signal of quality and safety for her child. And she went from awareness to purchase in less than our ninety-second moment. A moment was designed for her and the wee little one. It was elegant, engaging, and valuable for them as well as Neil's fledgling new corporation.

REMEMBER THE GOOD OL' DAYS? NOPE

CONCLUDING MEMORIES

CREATING STRONG MEMORIES IS ONLY HALF THE BATTLE. TRANSLATING MEMORIES INTO BRAND ENERGY AND CONVERTING THAT ENERGY TO SALES, PROFITS, AND BRAND VALUE IS THE OTHER HALF OF OUR JACOB'S LADDER MODEL FROM CHAPTER 1. THE DANCE OF DECISIONS BY THE PERSON AND THE BRAND OWNER IS CERTAINLY NOT A DANCE YOU LEARN READING *DANCING FOR DUMMIES*.

IF YOU WERE PAYING PROPER ATTENTION AND PERHAPS FLAGGING THE THOUGHTS YOU FOUND MOST INTERESTING, YOU'VE LIKELY TAKEN AWAY THESE LARGER BITS OF KNOWLEDGE:

1. Energy and utility are fuzzy concepts, but helpful to understand customer behavior. Energy is accumulated and spread from a person to her community. Like love or the Higgs boson, we know brand energy exits; it's just hard to measure.

2. Positive or negative shocks to brand energy may happen when positive or negative experiences (moments) occur.

3. Expected utility from personal use, utility from the social aspects of the experience, expected risk, price, and the cost of time to decide all seem to factor into the person's motivation to make a purchase.

4. Psychologists, economists, and others specialize in trying to understand the ultimate purchase decision-making process of the person. Sand in the gears occurs when decisions do not appear to be rational, which is often.

5. Brand owners have to decide how to design an offering, invest in branding, price, and maneuver around competitors. The combined results of these owner decisions and the customer decisions will determine the value created and the portion of the value that the owner keeps as brand value.

6. Unknowns and randomness impact the decisions of brand owners, handlers, community, and individuals.

08

SYSTEMS + VALUE

TO KNOW BEAUTY, YOU NEED TO SEE UGLY; TO KNOW BRANDS, YOU'LL HAVE TO EXPLORE GENERICS. IN THIS CHAPTER, WE'LL SPEND SOME TIME WITH BIG G AND WITH LITTLE G (GENERIC) FOOD COMPANIES WHERE NOURISHMENT COMES UNBRANDED. WE TAKE A PEEK UNDER THE HOOD OF A SOFTWARE TOOL THAT REVEALS THE INNER MECHANICS OF BRANDS MOVING THROUGH TIME AND SPACE. THE INSIGHT: WE SEE HOW BRANDS DELIVER VALUE TO PEOPLE AND BRAND OWNERS. THIS LEADS TO A SWAN DIVE (OR BELLY FLOP, DEPENDING ON YOUR PERSPECTIVE) INTO THE FINANCIAL WORLD OF GENERALLY ACCEPTED ACCOUNTING PRINCIPLES, INTANGIBLE ASSETS, AND RETURN ON BRANDING INVESTMENT. PUSH THROUGH; THIS IS THE CHAPTER YOU MAY NEED TO READ TWICE. IT'S OKAY. THIS IS ALSO A GOOD TIME TO BEGIN THINKING ABOUT YOUR CFO'S BIRTHDAY PRESENT. IT'S THE LEAST YOU CAN DO TO THANK HER FOR THE ABNORMALLY LARGE BONUS CHECK.

A SELFIE WITH YOUR NEW BESTIE, MS. CFO

FINANCIAL VALUE OF MARKETING

Here comes Linda the CFO, you know the clicking sound of her stilettos, a six-foot-tall force of financial intimidation and suffering. You know why she is coming, and the churning in your gut starts at the first click in the hallway. You've put together your branding-budget requests to achieve the growth goals for this next fiscal year and you're certain she is coming to ink your world in red.

She gets to your door and enters without a hello. The conversation is nothing but a question and tone packed to the gills with bias: "How do you expect me to support your budget request for the next fiscal year's marketing expenses?" You've used every trick in the book over the past ten years and you're considering recycling the less than adequate line, "You've got to spend money to make money, Linda." But you hesitate. It will certainly sound flippant and snarky. She drops the twenty-page, well-crafted "deck" on your desk with a large red question mark and leaves. It's Friday, long past beer o'clock.

Your weekend is occupied updating your LinkedIn page and pouring through your tattered marketing textbooks to review those classic advertising diffusion models from grad school. There has to be a better way to show Linda "the chief fear officer" the potential return on the budget you've requested. After some sweating, you pull in some geeks who can handle heavy statistical work and coding. But the noise in the data and time lags from past investments contributing to each period's profits are challenging. You're unable unpack the benefits with any acceptable degree of statistical confidence. What is wrong with these old advertising diffusion models?

At this point, you're falling back to saying you just know that marketing investment is good to do and you enlist the CMO to ask the CEO to get the CFO—and all accountants in general—out of marketing. But later on Monday, while napping on your desk, you dream about a new perspective on how brands gain energy. You intuitively know it can't be the same as it once was; too many things have changed in technology, culture, and our communities. There have to be new models out there in the world, right? Of course, like many wonderful dreams, just as you're going to download the formulas to a flash drive, the intern walks in and wakes you up.

Well there is a new diffusion model, and this chapter explores it. This means there's a way to show Linda some numbers capable of making her heart flutter. The first piece to understand is a use of micro-relationship data to give insight into macro-relationships. We'll start with a case study that goes deep into the wheat fields of South Dakota.

MORE WHEATIES, PLEASE

BIG G AND BRAND VALUE

You have wound your way through brands, brains, social networks, visual language, complex ideas, and likely a few nefarious paper cuts along the way. You're here patiently waiting for the big gift under the tree, answering the question, "How does this all come together?" You've learned about the many moving parts of a systems theory of brand. If you have jumped ahead to land here, welcome aboard, cheater. We hope you enjoy the ride.

In the following pages we unpack Aurora, a computer simulation tool that uses math, physics, and finance. But don't worry; this really isn't rocket science, though it does have a few equations used in the making of rockets. Most of these equations are already in use by researchers in the areas of marketing, economics, finance, social network theory, and elsewhere. Our contribution is to assemble the geared wheels, pinions, regulator, and springs into an end-to-end system that illustrates a brand moving through time and space.

We think you'll agree that the elements of our brand system are necessary, and that interesting outcomes emerge from interactions between these elements in the macro system. These elements include the Jacob's Ladder model and the Space Dimensions model. Both capture the micro-behaviors of people responding to brand owner investments. Memories and brand energy are shared with communities through time. The outputs include macro-behavior at the top rungs of Jacob's Ladder—sales, profits, and brand value—revealing the return on branding investments.

Half a century ago, a brand owner primarily relied on macro-behavior: Turn the wheel of advertising and wait to see if sales and profits follow. And even then, it was almost impossible to correlate cause with effect, which led advertising pioneer John Wanamaker to supposedly say, "Half the money I spend on advertising is wasted; the trouble is, I don't know which half." The invisible hand was, in fact, invisible. Today, brand owners can trace micro-behavior through click-stream, social media, point of sale, smartphone, and other means.

OUR BRAND SYSTEM SIMULATION IS CURRENTLY USED TO ILLUSTRATE WHY BRANDS ADD VALUE. IT CAN BE CALIBRATED AND TAILORED TO UNDERSTAND A SPECIFIC INDUSTRY, CATEGORY, AND INDIVIDUAL SETS OF BRANDS.

MY, OH MY! YOU'RE A BIG DOUGHBOY

GENERAL MILLS ACQUIRES PILLSBURY

To introduce our brand system model, we will loosely model the branded food industry and try to explain how the market values different players and the different ways that brands in that industry add value. First, we'll use the example of General Mills from our case study at the end of Chapter 2 (see Why Wheaties Are Made of Gold: General Mills Case Study). In 2000, the Big G Cereal brands' sales were around 40 percent of General Mills's $6.7 billion total revenue, sharing space with Gold Medal Flour, Betty Crocker, and other iconic brands. General Mills's investment in tangible assets such as factories and inventory was about $2.3 billion, but the market valued its assets at around $14 billion (Linda the CFO would call this the market value of investment capital, or MVIC), about six times the book value of its tangible assets. Why the difference? If an appraisal of its factories and inventory had been done, there could have been some appreciation in their values, perhaps explaining a 25 percent to 50 percent increase, because land values had gone up in some places and repairs had kept the equipment going longer.

That leaves about $10 billion of unaccounted-for added value. Well, to be more precise, about $0.5 billion was "accounted for" on General Mills's balance sheet as intangible assets that had been recognized in the acquisitions of Lloyd's Barbeque, Small Planet Foods, Yoplait, and others. However, all investments in the Big G brands such as the sponsorship payments to Tiger Woods, radio and TV spots, promotional coupons, etc., had been expensed as they were incurred, so there is no "value" for the Big G brands on General Mills's balance sheet. Curiously, build a brand inside and you don't need to account for it; acquire a brand and you'll need to account for it.

Then along comes the announcement in mid-2000 that General Mills was going to spend around $10 billion to double its sales by buying the milling company on the other side of the Mississippi—the Pillsbury Doughboy. That deal took two years to complete and $1 billion of assets were sold again for antitrust reasons, after which management took on the task of appraising the assets acquired. Tangible asset appraisals came in at a total of $0.7 billion, brand assets at $3.1 billion after some related deferred taxes, and goodwill was $5.2 billion. The total intangible assets (brand and goodwill) were $8.3 billion, over eleven times the value of the tangible assets. This is a "yowza" dollar amount for intangibles.

So a brand that is built organically has no asset value on the owner's balance sheet, but the market knows the brand has value. Also a brand's value can be many times the value of the tangible assets that are used to manufacture and deliver the product. It is commonly said that intangible assets are 80 percent or more of today's U.S. economic assets versus only 20 percent in the heavy industry days of the early 1980s. So Wall Street is in the intangible asset business, essentially. In the case of Pillsbury, a whopping 92 percent of its total value when it was purchased was deemed to come from intangible assets. We'll get into the issues of what is brand value versus goodwill later on.

GOING WHERE BRANDS DON'T SURVIVE

THE UNDERBRANDED WORLD

Contrast this branded-food business with a commodity-food business that buys, processes, and sells wheat, soybeans, corn, and other food staples. All competitors in this space sell the same products using the same grading system, so there is no discernable difference in quality between competitors; only price and availability matter.

In this nonbranded world, producers will still make sales and profits. Customers will still realize utility from their bag of flour or gallon of corn oil. Since customers concern themselves only with price, keeping track of whose bag they bought last week doesn't matter. This is a direct application of our earlier thought experiment in which customers have no memory and there are no brands. Archer Daniels Midland (ADM) and Bunge are publicly traded examples of these types of commodity food companies. The stock market values their assets at around 1.0 to 1.5 times their book value of tangible assets. Brand value is minimal or nonexistent. No need to remember a brand that has no brand value.

Seneca Foods operates further up the food chain by processing fruit and vegetables into canned, bottled, and frozen product. Over half of its sales are private label (i.e., generic) products sold to grocery retailers. According to SenecaFood.com, about 13 percent is from being a contract manufacturer for General Mills's Green Giant branded product, and Seneca's own branded products such as Libby make up only 12 percent of its total sales. Seneca has been valued by the market at just under one times its book value of tangible assets throughout the last decade, which suggests that the market gives it little or no credit for having brand assets.

So why do General Mills brands have value? In their annual filings with the Securities and Exchange Commission, they say:

"The value of our brands is based in large part on the degree to which consumers react and respond positively to these brands. Brand value could diminish significantly due to a number of factors, including consumer perception that we have acted in an irresponsible manner, adverse publicity about our products, our failure to maintain the quality of our products, the failure of our products to deliver consistently positive consumer experiences, concerns about food safety, or our products becoming unavailable to consumers."

General Mills considers consistent quality and safety as key to brand value in the market segment they serve within this product category. This is seconded by a former member of the Financial Accounting Standards Board, Edward Trott. Trott notes in the May 2015 issue of *CFO* magazine, "When you open a box of Cheerios you know what to expect. This consistency is part of what makes the Cheerios brand valuable." In Chapter 7, we talked about the multiple ways that brands provide value to the customer. Risk reduction is one of those ways. Thank you General Mills for reinforcing our point to our readers and your investors.

A brand's ability to reduce risk works in several ways: It can guide customers to repeat positive experiences after a customer finds a good match with his or her innate preferences. It also allows a customer to remember his or her personal history of brand experiences and to use those memories to avoid brands that aren't a good match with innate preferences and brands with intolerable quality control.

Finally, quality allows customers who are risk averse to benefit from learning about experiences of those in their community who are less concerned about risk. Risk tolerance varies from person to person, and the degree of risk tolerance changes from one product category to the next. The average risk tolerance for inconsistent quality in tissue paper may be greater than the tolerance for inconsistent pacemakers.

THE FLOW OF HEAT, SLOWED WAY DOWN

A GLIMPSE INSIDE AURORA

Aurora is a computer program that calculates dozens of brand variables through advanced formulas to model existing reality and develop future scenarios. The variables we use are more diverse than the variables typically used to study brands today, and are influenced by the content of this book.

No two brand situations are the same, so you

FIGURE 8.1: AURORA'S INSTRUMENT PANEL

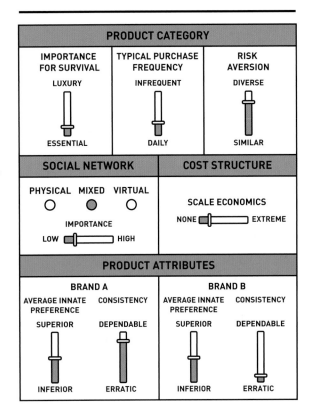

Aurora's instrument panel specifies the brand's industry environment that affects the ability for a brand to add value.

need to use the best available evidence to develop branding strategies and evaluate brand value. Using one common formula or a black-box model with hidden data will have limited usefulness and questionable applicability to inform branding decisions or evaluate brand value. The system needs to be open. Aurora makes the variables, assumptions, and formulas explicit and known.

Since space moves through time, Aurora feeds the results of current-period calculations of interactions in space forward in time as a dynamic system that can replay time with hundreds or thousands of simulations. Additionally, since human beings buy brands, the foundation of our simulation begins with the attributes and decisions of the person.

For our first glimpse deeper inside Aurora, we will use the controls in the instrument panel shown in Figure 8.1 and select key attributes to illustrate the risk-reduction benefits between General Mills's branded products and Seneca's generic products. We have identified a wide variety of potential controls, many of which could lead to brand value in one industry but not another. Just as brands cater to different people, we believe brand value comes from different sources depending on the brand.

The branded food competitor is modeled as Brand A and the generic food processor is Brand B. As shown in the top block, there is a diversity of attitudes toward risk, where some customers are highly concerned with quality and others are less concerned. This product category is a frequent purchase and not considered a luxury. The community includes both physical and virtual social networks, but the importance of social during consumption is fairly low. While the community can still share information on experiences, it has little impact on the utility the person experiences when consuming the product, despite the suggestion that Wheaties eaters belong to a tribe of "Champions."

Both Brand A and B have similar manufacturing and distribution cost structures. In the bottom block, we specify that although the people in this model have a range of innate preferences toward each brand, the average customer utility from the sensory experience of consuming each brand is the same. However, the branded product has a more consistent quality. Another set of instruments allows us to specify the type of branding investment the parties would make. The branded product conducts branding activities but the generic food processor does not.

With these inputs, we assign values to each computer-simulated person in the network. These include each person's innate preferences toward each brand, sensitivity to risk, and the strengths of connections with other nodes that have the effect of defining communities. Then the simulation begins with the brand owners making their brand investments, and then setting a price for their products for that period in an attempt to maximize profits with whatever information they have collected in prior periods.

People then apply trust apertures to block some of the incoming energy from brand investments, and then weigh what they know about each brand (which is nothing in the first period) against the perceived risk for each brand and choose the product that they expect will give them the most utility for the price. The perceived risk of each brand relates to expected product quality and the risk of customers not fully knowing their innate preference for the brand prior to their first experience.

Once customers accumulate experiences by buying and experiencing a brand, a range of experienced utility from the product informs future purchases. Accumulated experiences, if positive, build trust in the brand owner, so apertures to owner signals dilate and give these signals more influence. Once owners have seen the effects of changes in quantities sold from their pricing decisions, owners get better at setting prices to maximize profits. The owners that sell larger quantities realize a lower fixed cost, which makes them more profitable.

Brand energy is a key driver of the model, similar to petroleum in an internal combustion engine. At first, the effects of branding investments help pump up brand energy by increasing expected utility and decreasing expected risk. If these expectations lead to purchasing the product, customers find out what the experience is like. If the experience meets or exceeds expectations, energy gets a bump. Customers will also share their energy with their community and vice versa. Our models show that most of the energy emanates from the experiences of using the brand—a central insight.

If their community feels a new brand is superior to old brands, word will spread and brand energy will increase. At the end of each period, customers will suffer some memory loss based on the half-life of the sensory source of the memories. We repeat this process many times until the system enters into a steady-state market share, price, profit, and brand value to each owner.

Because of randomness in individual experiences, each scenario from a given product category will result in slightly different results.

THOUGHT EXPERIMENT

IF ALL OF YOUR PRODUCT-CATEGORY CUSTOMERS WERE SUDDENLY AMNESIACS, HOW WOULD THAT CHANGE YOUR STRATEGY?

If we run hundreds or thousands of scenarios with the same initial setup, we can quantify the average and range of outcomes. If an entrepreneur's life were like Bill Murray's in *Groundhog Day*, we could restart a brand's journey many times over and discover the real risk owners and brand managers face. Unfortunately, repeatable experiments are a luxury available to physical scientists, not to social scientists. The goal is to create a model that produces a scenario matching what we actually see, and to explore other scenarios to give insight into what could also have happened.

Understand that this is a computer simulation based upon general conceptual relationships and requires assumptions for the forms and parameters of many equations. We have drawn from academic literature and empirical studies, but some areas need more study. Further, each equation may be brand and product-category specific. Serious side effects may occur. Consult your doctor if you experience excessive dizziness or heart palpitations due to excessive happiness or excitement.

HEY SEXY NUMBERS, HOW YOU DOING?

A NEW DIFFUSION MODEL

Figure 8.2 is a summary of the results from the branded versus generic food world: Most roads point to a final steady-state branded product's market share of around 84 percent, which is the result of a 77 percent share of units sold and a price premium of 26 percent. This is in line with the IRI 2015 consumer packaged-goods industry survey that says national brands have an average of 83 percent of their product category market share and a 24 percent price premium over generics. Aurora helps explain why this could happen.

We can capture a more extreme version of an unbranded world by forcing a complete memory loss from one period to the next. In this world, Brand A achieves a market share of only 50 percent and fails to achieve a price premium, despite Brand A's branding investment.

As expected, competition is only based upon price, and these companies drive prices and profits down to only provide a return on their tangible assets. This shows the importance of making the moments and memories that build a brand.

Back to the branded versus generic food world, Figure 8.3 shows the breakdown of the final period's unit sales price relative to the generic price, cost of sales, branding investment, and profits. Notice that the generic brand is still a brand and commands higher prices and profits than the no-memory results.

Figure 8.4 shows the branded versus generic world market shares over time. Since these converge to a steady state, we can project after-tax profits and cash flows after the final period. This means we can value the brands at the end of the simulation. Figure 8.5 shows the accounting and valuation results in the language that Linda the CFO would understand.

Drum roll please: the branded product is worth over nine times the value of the tangible assets used to produce it. This is not unlike the value of our poster child brand portfolio company, General Mills, which was valued by the market at 8.6 times its tangible assets at the end of 2014. This implies that its intangibles were worth nearly $40 billion.

The no-memory world implies that the unbranded product line is only worth the value of its tangible assets. The generic "brand" is worth four times its tangible assets, so it actually has some intangible value. This makes sense since some people discover that they favor the generic because of its lower price, their insensitivity to risk, or their innate preferences.

DO IT TILL YOU REACH DIMINISHING RETURNS

HOW MUCH TO SPEND?

You will notice that the generic brand makes no branding investment. If we rerun the model to also set the branded product's investment to zero,

FIGURE 8.2: PRICE PREMIUM & MARKET SHARE

523 SIMULATIONS

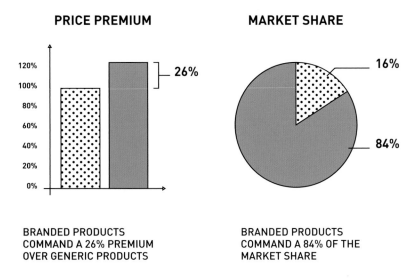

PRICE PREMIUM

MARKET SHARE

BRANDED PRODUCTS COMMAND A 26% PREMIUM OVER GENERIC PRODUCTS

BRANDED PRODUCTS COMMAND A 84% OF THE MARKET SHARE

▨ **BRANDED**   ⬚ **GENERIC**

In this simulation the branded product has superior consistency, which is rewarded with a price premium and larger market share. These figures are the average result of 523 simulations. Randomness, viral behavior, and other events cause each simulation to vary from the other.

FIGURE 8.3: COST ELEMENTS

523 SIMULATIONS

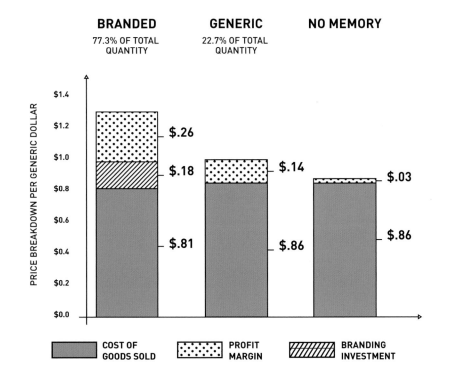

BRANDED
77.3% OF TOTAL QUANTITY

GENERIC
22.7% OF TOTAL QUANTITY

NO MEMORY

▨ **COST OF GOODS SOLD**   ⬚ **PROFIT MARGIN**   ⧄ **BRANDING INVESTMENT**

The branded product's branding investment is more than offset by a higher price and lower cost relative to the generic product. In contrast, when there is no memory, competitors drive profits to the point where they only provide the required return on the tangible assets used to manufacture and distribute the product.

FIGURE 8.4: AVERAGE MARKET SHARE

523 SIMULATIONS

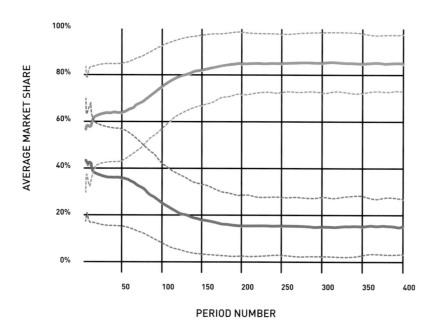

GENERIC — BRANDED

* DASHED LINES REPRESENT +/- ONE STANDARD DEVIATION FROM THE MEAN

In the branded versus generic world, the branded product quickly achieves a dominant market share. The time path of market shares differ from scenario to scenario because of randomness in product quality, which product each of the 10,000 simulated people buys first, and other factors. The variations in this time path are summarized by the band around the middle path. This is the time dimension of the brand moving through time and space.

FIGURE 8.5: TANGIBLE ASSET MULTIPLES

RATIO OF MARKET VALUE OF INVESTED CAPITAL TO TANGIBLE ASSETS

	BRANDED	GENERIC	NO MEMORY
REVENUE	$1.26	$1.00	$0.89
AFTER-TAX PROFIT MARGIN	14.5%	9.5%	2.2%
AFTER-TAX PROFIT	$0.18	$0.09	$0.02
IMPLIED MVIC	$4.67	$2.15	$0.45
MVIC/ TANGIBLE ASSETS	9.3X	4.3X	0.9X

The branded company is worth over 9 times the value of its tangible assets, similar to General Mills. The generic brand has more value than the no-memory world. Some people just prefer the plain product. Go figure.

we can isolate the benefit that branding has on the final brand value in the scenario when there is marketing investment. Without branding investment, the branded product's consistent quality is still discovered by those that have tried and repeated purchasing the product. Energy is then shared throughout the community by word of mouth. This is, essentially, free branding investment and acts to leverage an owner's investment in scenarios when they do invest. This free branding investment also occurs to some extent for the "generic" brand in this model for the persons that innately prefer the generic.

In the world with no owner investment, Brand A's steady-state market share is 73 percent and price premium is 5 percent. Although Brand A eliminates the expense of its branding investment, the reductions in price and market share more than offset the branding reductions, so total profits are 48 percent lower in each period. If we just look at the steady-state branding investment versus profit enhancement in the final period, the return on that investment is 57 percent of the investment.

Yes, we know what you're thinking. What happens if we double our investment? Does that double the steady-state return? Is there an extreme case when marketing investment becomes nearly 100 percent of sales and Brand A's profit and loss statement is bleeding red?

Figure 8.6 shows the results of moving this investment lever from zero to the point of negative return and shows that, in fact, there is an optimal level of marketing investment, and after that, you are dropping money into an overflowing porta-potty.

Another illustration of the effects of branding investment is to start with the no-investment world, and then, after it has entered a steady state, invest for only a short period. Let's call this a single marketing investment pulse.

The results are shown in Figure 8.7. The immediate response to the single pulse (A) is an increase in energy (B). This leads to new-customer first purchases, repeated experiences, and more discoveries of the greater product consistency of Brand A. Energy spreads to the communities of these new happy customers.

This slowly translates into a rise in sales, prices (C) and profits (D), ultimately settling

FIGURE 8.6: OPTIMAL LEVEL OF INVESTMENT

PERCENT PROFIT INCREASE OVER NO INVESTMENT SCENARIO

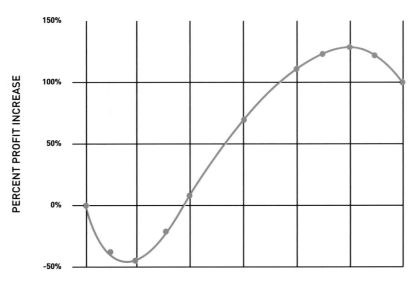

PERCENT PROFIT INCREASE

BRANDING INVESTMENT

No, this is not a Nike swoosh. This shows how the return on branding investment depends upon the level of investment. At low levels of investment, there is no customer response, but you're still out your investment. The top of the hump is the profit-maximizing investment level. After that, you're throwing good money after bad.

FIGURE 8.7: BRAND IMPULSE RESPONSE

100 SIMULATIONS

A: BRAND ENERGY INVESTMENT

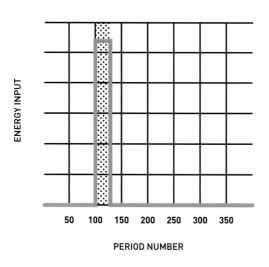

C: PRICE INCREASE

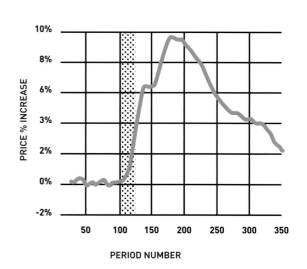

B: TOTAL BRAND ENERGY

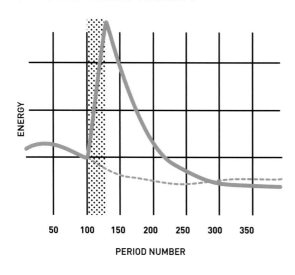

D: PERIOD PROFIT INCREASE

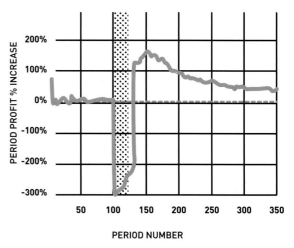

- - - - - - - - - - **NO BRANDING INVESTMENT**　　　　　　　　　**PULSE OF BRANDING INVESTMENT**

The effect of a single pulse of branding investment (A) boosts brand energy (B), which slowly decays again.
When the energy peaks, the brand owner discovers it can maximize its profits by raising prices (C) for a while without
losing too much volume. Some of this profit enhancement continues through the end of the simulated time (D).

in at a permanently higher level than the no-investment world. The differences between these two worlds lead to the unpacking of the returns to a single marketing investment. In the language of systems theory, this is called an impulse response function. In the world of business, one pulse of branding is not optimal.

NOTHING TO PERFECTION

ONE END OF THE SPECTRUM AND BACK

When a customer makes a purchase, the difference between his utility and the price paid is referred to as consumer surplus. In other words, some customers who have bought a brand would have been willing to pay more, but since we are forcing the producers to set a single price for all customers, those that would have paid more get to keep the difference as consumer surplus. The combination of owner profits and consumer surplus is called social welfare.

When we add memory and a brand to the no-memory world, the total social welfare increases. Since total social welfare increased in the branded world, the mere existence of brands has added value, but the owners only captured a small portion. If these brand owners were able to charge different prices to groups of customers the way airlines price seats, then the owners could capture a greater share of the social welfare.

We can also consider the thought experiment of what would happen in the branded versus generic world if all the players had perfect information. Without perfect information, owners and people try to discover their best product match and price. It is inevitable that some people will stay with their original choice rather than trying all brands because of their aversion to risk and, as a result, will not discover the brand that suits them best. Likewise, a brand could be mispriced or directed at the wrong audience and miss out on connecting with raving fans. Since we can be the gods of this imaginary world, we know what product each person would choose and the price and market share that each brand owner would

achieve if everyone knew everything. This gives us a benchmark of potential brand value and can be compared against each brand owner's branding investment strategy and ultimate brand value in the imperfect information world.

In the branded versus generic food world with perfect information, Brand A would have a market share of 95 percent, a price premium of 21 percent, and a brand value of $23.8 billion. That means that the Brand A imperfect world value of $4.67 billion in Figure 8.5 is only 20 percent of the potential value. Having the ability to model potential versus actual brand value is new, with exciting applications.

Let's consider a different branding strategy. Instead of a constant level of marketing investment, let Brand A pulse with branding energy at twice the former level for thirty periods (days) and zero for the next month so that the total investment remains unchanged, as depicted in Figure 8.8.

This strategy results in a 55 percent increase in value over the constant investment strategy for Brand A. The efficiency of a pulsing investment strategy is a well-known phenomenon in the world of advertising and has been statistically analyzed by academics using actual frozen food product category point-of-sale data. Their findings attribute effectiveness of pulsing to the carryover effect of advertising into future periods (in other words, memory), as well as the assumed shape of the customer utility function. It is likely that this strategy will also work in a post-brand-advertising world.

Another perhaps subtle result from this pulsing strategy is that the potential value from the perfect-world scenario has increased slightly. This is because we have modeled a person's expected utility to depend in part upon the change in brand energy since the past period. Since branding investment injects energy into the system, memory decays more slowly, making customers ever more hopeful that the next consumption experience will be even better than past experiences. Although this seems irrational, there is evidence to support this positive outlook bias, as discussed in Chapter 6. It may be a partial

FIGURE 8.8: MARKETING INVESTMENT

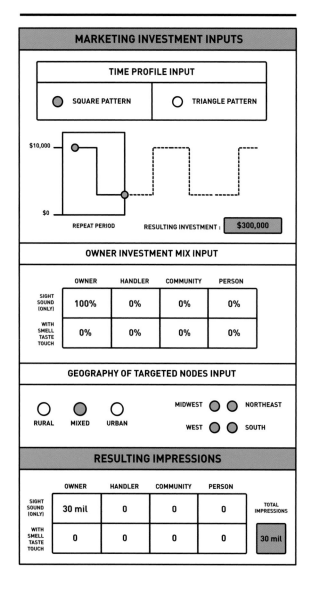

Aurora's instrument panel allows the brand owner to specify the branding investment over time and space. For now, we'll do only mass-media brand advertising, in which all investment originates from the owner and is turned into the sight and sound senses with a television commercial. This assumes a reachable and receptive market.

explanation for why universally known products such as Coca-Cola still engage in branding initiatives. Or it may be that further research could reveal a more complex relationship between energy and expected utility than the one we are using in this scenario.

Now what happens if the generic Brand B begins to invest in branding activities and also follows a pulsing strategy?

As shown in Figure 8.9, the effectiveness of Brand A's advertising strategy has been partially compromised by Brand B's competition in branding activities. The resulting market share for Brand A is reduced from over 80 percent to just over 60 percent.

This is where the game becomes fascinating, because the success of your own branding investment depends upon the other brands' chosen strategy. To figure out your optimal investment, you could put your resident mathematical wizards onto computing the Nash equilibrium equation that takes into account the fact that the competitors have their own mathematical wizards on deck. If you happen to be short a wizard, try military strategy and hope you can bluff or intimidate the other side into blinking.

A HIDDEN GATE INTO A MATURE MARKET

A NEW KIND OF SNACK BAR

Staying in the branded-food product pasture, how could a new brand succeed in entering into an already mature market competing against billion-dollar companies? Perhaps if it can find a secret passage to market success. But the odds would still be against it. We are talking about our example from Chapter 3 of the KIND Bar from KIND Healthy Snacks with its social mission to "make the world a little kinder." To address this, we introduce Brand C into Aurora's branded versus generic world after Brand A and Brand B are firmly entrenched. Brand C will have a higher average innate preference, higher product quality,

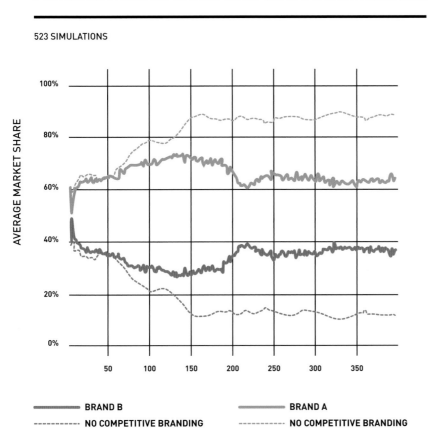

FIGURE 8.9: MARKET SHARE WITH COMPETITIVE BRANDING

523 SIMULATIONS

Here the generic product from Figure 8.4 turns into a branded product (Brand B) by investing in brand-building activities. As a result it takes market share from Brand A. The lesson: the results of Brand A's marketing investment depend on what its competitors do.

BRAND B
-------- NO COMPETITIVE BRANDING

BRAND A
-------- NO COMPETITIVE BRANDING

higher product cost, and higher social appeal. We also slide the social importance lever up, since KIND brought this issue to the category with its not-only-for-profit business model.

KIND launched with community events focused on rewarding kind acts for others and sending the message that consuming KIND products helps the community, which gives a boost to the customer's utility from the experience. Free samples are given out at these events. KIND's founder, Daniel Lubetzky, claims that 90 percent of people who try a free sample of a KIND Bar become hooked on the product. And brain research on the power of taste and smell supports this belief. KIND's clear packaging, free samples, and events involve the senses of touch, taste, and smell. To match this example, we use levers in Aurora to set Brand C's branding investment to include all senses and direct most of the investment toward community and individuals.

We have launched Brand C with the branding investment set at a constant level that is 15 percent higher than Brand A's levels. For most new brands, the capital to fund this level of investment would be unattainable. Since KIND's financial information is not publicly available, we've had to make some hypothetical assumptions for our illustrative world. The instrument panel translates the total budget into a number of brand engagements using a schedule of prices per engagement loosely based upon real data. This funding level results in fewer total engagements per period than Brand A achieved with its brand advertising strategy, because interacting directly with specific customers can be more costly than national advertising. On the other hand, the effectiveness of the investment is greater because the persons have a greater trust of their own experiences and energy received from their community than they would from an advertising promise by a distant brand.

Aurora's results from a specific scenario with a successful entrance by Brand C is shown in Figure 8.10.

Sales of Brand C start slowly soon after its launch (period 300), as a delayed reaction to the full-on launch of Brand C's marketing investment. The micro-level mechanisms that drive the delayed sales macro-behavior include the building of energy, the time carryovers due to memory, and "free" investment from the word of mouth spreading across the communities.

Brand C starts out priced above Brand A and only takes around 10 percent of the market. Around 250 periods after its launch, Brand C lowers its price to match Brand A for a short time, which causes more people to give it a try, and new rabid fans stay with Brand C even after it returns to its initial price. This results in a new steady-state market share of 30 percent. Brand A succeeds in retaining around 60 percent market share, compared to 90 percent or so share prior to C's entrance. Throughout most of the scenario, Brand C is priced at around a 10 percent premium to Brand A. Brand A's price remains relatively unchanged after C's entrance.

Interestingly, Aurora includes a rather simple pricing mechanism, in which brand owners continually update their estimates of the demand curve based upon the quantities they have won for the prices they set in earlier periods. In this particular scenario, the randomness in the data caused Brand C to drop its prices so it temporarily matched Brand A's price. Even though it quickly raised its prices again, many of the happy customers that had discovered that they prefer Brand C to Brand A, even at a higher price, stayed with C. This is not unlike KIND Bar's strategy of offering free samples, and claims that 90 percent of the people that try their product become loyal customers, despite its higher price. As we know, taste and smell memories run deep, and risk aversion is likely amplified in food products.

Figure 8.11 shows the average of the market shares when we include the results from 431

FIGURE 8.10: MARKET SHARE

SIMULATION 12 OF 432

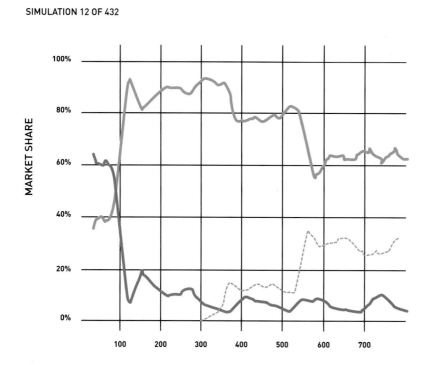

Simulation 12 of 432 simulations is a single scenario for a late competitor's entry. In this scenario, a temporary price reduction encourages first trial and creates raving fans that later stay with the new entrant once original pricing is restored.

more scenarios along with the scenario in Figure 8.10. On average, sales of Brand C start slowly soon after its launch, but follow an upward arc similar to those market penetration curves in the old-fashioned macro-level advertising diffusion models. Although, on average, about 20 percent share is won, this is not always a financial success.

Figure 8.12 shows all the paths of cumulative profits for the 432 simulations of Brand C's entrance. All start with losses while sales are slow in responding to the branding investment. Only about 20 percent have achieved positive cumulative profits by the last period. We have forced a shutdown in approximately 60 percent of the scenarios that reached more than $100,000 in cumulative losses. This percentage, by the way, is consistent with the typical survival rates of new ventures.

Figure 8.13 shows the range of total values implied by each scenario for the Brand C product launch. If we knew that these were all possible scenarios when deciding to invest in C, we would have weighted these scenarios to find that the expected value of Brand C was $1.3 billion, which is close to the value of the single successful outcome shown in Figure 8.10. However, as shown by the median on Figure 8.13, over half of the simulations resulted in failure and a financial loss. According to Nielson, the actual odds of a new brand offering in the consumer packaged-goods industry failing in the first two years is 85 percent.

On the other hand, approximately 20 percent of the simulations result in a value of over $3 billion and a select few even reach $5 billion. Nielson says that in 2012, only 2 percent of the new offerings had first-year sales of over $50 million. Remind you of being told to bet on "Lucky Dan to Place" in the movie *The Sting*? Were they meaning KIND's CEO Dan Lubetzky? It's easier to predict the future after the future has actually occurred.

We have a tendency to look to successes as a fait accompli after a successful brand launch (or after a technological success or a wildcat oil

FIGURE 8.11: AVERAGE MARKET SHARE

A summary of market shares from many scenarios for a late competitor's entry. On average, the new entrant achieves roughly 20% market share by period 800. This is not always a financial success.

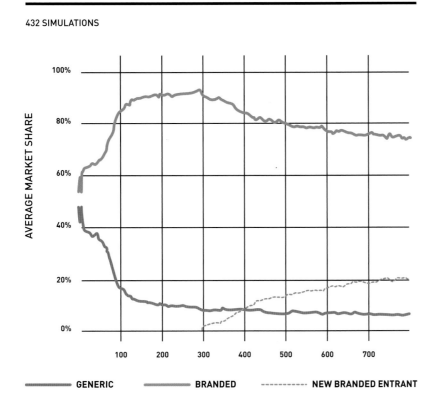

432 SIMULATIONS

GENERIC   BRANDED   NEW BRANDED ENTRANT

FIGURE 8.12: TOTAL PROFIT FOR NEW ENTRANT

432 SIMULATIONS

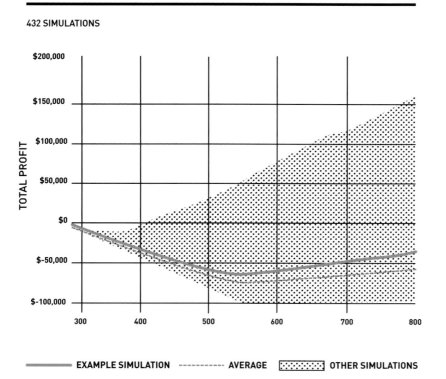

——— EXAMPLE SIMULATION - - - - - AVERAGE ▓▓▓ OTHER SIMULATIONS

A summary of profits from many scenarios for a later competitor's entry. Many scenarios have a cumulative loss in the 800th period, but some, such as the example simulation from Figure 8.10, will soon recoup its investment and have a cumulative net profit.

FIGURE 8.13: NEW ENTRANT VALUE

432 SIMULATIONS

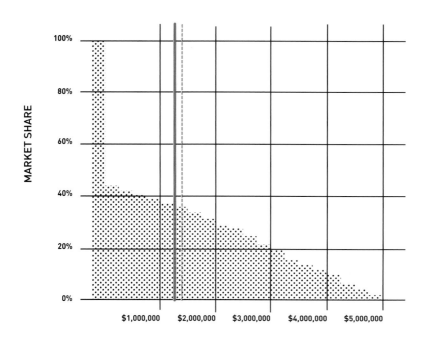

——— EXPECTED VALUE - - - - - SAMPLE SIMULATION

A summary of brand valuations from many scenarios for a late competitor's entry. More than half are worthless. Late entry is risky. You might want to buy an existing brand rather than create a new one.

strike), because we rarely have information to quantify the true risk that was faced. One method to value an early-stage brand hopeful is to look at how the market has valued other brand hopefuls at a similar stage. Unfortunately, looking for data on comparable early-stage companies that are publicly traded can be an exercise in hunting for unicorns. Instead, appraisers will develop projections similar to Aurora's simulations or use techniques that are used to value stock options. Stock option pricing methods also implicitly assume a range of possible scenarios.

RANDOM SHOCKS IN A DIGITAL WORLD

YOUR WORST NIGHTMARE

If you are a brand manager, you might have paid more attention to the first part of the General Mills annual statement quote we previously mentioned since you've probably lost some shut-eye for fear of negative events becoming your brand story as well. We'll repeat it here just to torture you further: "Brand value could diminish significantly due to a number of factors, including consumer perception that we have acted in an irresponsible manner, adverse publicity about our products . . ." The original quote goes even further: "The growing use of social and digital media by consumers, us, and third parties increases the speed and extent that information or misinformation and opinions can be shared. Negative posts or comments about us, our brands, or our products on social or digital media could seriously damage our brands and reputation. If we do not maintain the favorable perception of our brands, our business results could be negatively impacted." This addresses the brave new world of branding.

General Mills's competition, KIND Healthy Snacks, has recently had its own adverse publicity challenges. In March of 2015, the Food and Drug Administration (FDA) issued a public letter stating: "Dear Mr. Lubetsky" (their misspelling), and continuing, "none of your products listed above meet the requirements for use of the nutrient content claim 'healthy' that are set forth in 21 CFR 101.65(d)(2)." Kick in the teeth for a company whose name includes the word *healthy*. General Mills has had its own share of similar letters such as the FDA's challenge to its labeling of Cheerios as "cholesterol lowering." In its early days, KIND benefited from the FDA's small-business exemption for products selling less than 10,000 units per year.

Our model includes a random variable added to the utility realized with each person's experience of a product, which we attribute to product quality inconsistencies. There is also randomness in the energy imparted by brand handlers. While an owner can try to influence a handler such as granting an interview to news media, there is a risk that the end result introduces negative energy. Some handlers, such as the FDA, will target a brand in a positive or negative way without the owner's involvement. So much for "free" marketing investment when the effect is negative. This supports the old marketing maxim, "Nothing kills a bad product quicker than good advertising." A similar, but more geographically focused, negative energy can originate from a customer who, by chance, experiences several negative experiences when consuming a brand and creates a hater website with a large social media following.

Aurora's virtual scale-free social networks occasionally give us a glimpse of viral behavior erupting on a national scale. While actual social network relationships can be observed through social media sites and elsewhere, the math we use to create random social communities is a rough approximation of communities that exist in the real world. When we introduce a positive or negative random shock from either a brand handler or from consecutive positive or negative customer utility experiences, we can sometimes see that information spread through the nodes.

Figure 8.14 shows how an energy input toward Brand A (positive or negative) can diffuse across the network. In this particular example, the nodes are only connected geographically, where each node is connected only to its nearest neighbors.

THOUGHT EXPERIMENT

WHAT ELSE WOULD YOU NEED TO KNOW ABOUT YOUR CURRENT AND POTENTIAL CUSTOMERS AND COMPETITORS TO ACHIEVE YOUR BRAND'S FULL POTENTIAL VALUE?

In the first map, a customer located in the San Francisco area receives a positive energy input, perhaps from a positive experience with the brand. In the following maps, it is possible to see this energy diffuse across the country as each node shares its experience with the brand with its network of friends, eventually reaching as far as the Mississippi River. The impulse response in time was already discussed; this is the impulse response in space. If we add the scale-free distribution, energy spreads virtually and physically, so can move even faster. Hello velocity!

Remember, both positive and negative energy can spread through the network. The effects of negative energy spread by a handler, such as the FDA, are more widespread, as the input is received by many individuals spread throughout the network at the same time. In that case, many nodes are impacted throughout the map and the persons with the strongest and greatest number of connections effectively relay that negative energy to their communities. This is the nightmare scenario. If you have a social media team supporting your brand, you may have seen something like this happen in real-time data. We hope, for your sake, you were seeing results from the spread of a positive energy boost.

A BIG GAAP IN YOUR GOODWILL

CONTRASTING GOODWILL AND INTANGIBLES

Most of the brand asset evaluation methods published in popular culture fail to meet the "non-black-box" requirements of the U.S. Generally Accepted Accounting Principles (GAAP). This is part of the reason we wanted to discuss the distinction between goodwill and brand intangible assets.

Accounting guidance under GAAP defines goodwill as "an asset representing the future economic benefits arising from other assets acquired in a business combination that are not individually identified and separately recognized." We know your next thought: "What the?" It is

LARGER PLAYER, LARGER SCRUTINY

THE SMALL-BUSINESS EXEMPTION FOR PRODUCTS SAYS, "IF A PERSON IS NOT AN IMPORTER, AND HAS FEWER THAN 10 FULL-TIME EQUIVALENT EMPLOYEES, THAT PERSON DOES NOT HAVE TO FILE A NOTICE FOR ANY FOOD PRODUCT WITH ANNUAL SALES OF FEWER THAN 10,000 TOTAL UNITS."

measured as the difference between the total purchase price to acquire a business and the sum of the value of the individual assets. This is also referred to as the residual method, or, in less technical terms, "the accountant's junk drawer." Conceptually, goodwill includes value for the assembled workforce, synergies that two companies can realize if joined together, and future assets that a business is expected to create such as new technologies and new products. It's the business system.

So we're going to dig into that junk drawer and sort through the items that matter to the brand manager. The assets you may consider to be a part of a brand might be recognized as several assets under GAAP if the business is acquired. Examples of these are trade names, trademarks, domain names, customer relationships, design patents, and utility patents. As for calling it a brand asset, accounting guidance from FASB Accounting Standards Codification says, "The terms *brand* and *brand name*, often used as synonyms for trademarks and other marks, are general marketing terms that typically refer to a group of complementary assets such as a trademark (or service mark) and its related trade name, formulas, recipes, and technological expertise. This Statement does not preclude an entity from recognizing, as a single asset separately from goodwill, a group of complementary intangible assets commonly

FIGURE 8.14: GEOGRAPHIC SPREADING

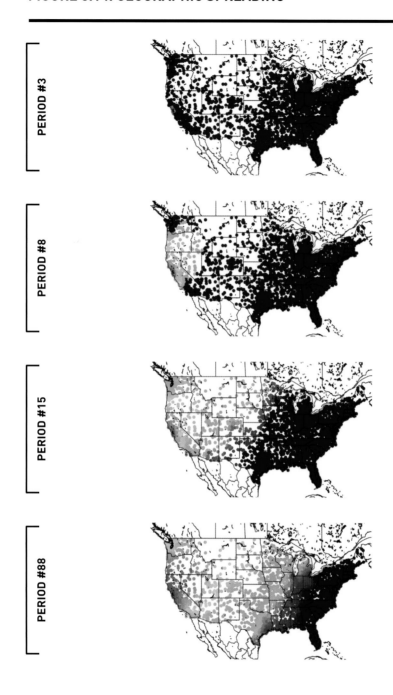

PERIOD #3

PERIOD #8

PERIOD #15

PERIOD #88

Every brand's dream—to spread like the flu.

referred to as a brand if the assets that make up that group have similar useful lives." So, go ahead, you have permission to tell your CFO to call the bundle of assets you oversee a big ol' beautiful brand asset.

So where do you draw the line between brand asset and goodwill? This has to do with what portion of projected future revenues and profits from the company relate to the brand. Appraisers often use a royalty rate for the use of the brand's trade name using comparable publicly disclosed license agreements. The challenge here is the license agreements for trade names and trademarks are often for complementary products or undeveloped territories. No sane brand owner licenses its brand to a competitor selling a highly comparable offering.

Another appraisal approach is to estimate the portion of the total product profit that comes from the use of your brand name. The low-hanging fruit in this estimate is to compare the price premium the brand commands over generic products. We saw that in our branded versus generic food world. If you stopped using the brand name, you would definitely give up that premium. But what market share of the quantities sold would you also give up? The profits from some of that additional market share belong to the value of the brand as well.

Another consideration that we see with General Mills in particular is that the brands offer stickiness in a category and defense against the competitive business cycle. This gives them a lower cost of equity capital. It also allows them to use their brands as collateral in raising debt capital far in excess of their tangible assets. Not all brands are this fortunate, but it certainly helps General Mills in achieving the market asset value to tangible book value multiple we see.

The distinction between what is brand versus goodwill should relate to the economic substance of a company and its brands. Like many things in life, following a standard formula may lead to illogical results. As an illustration—without knowing the specifics—we recently analyzed an $80 million snack brand line acquired by a public company where $30 million was allocated to brand assets, $48 million to goodwill, and less than $2 million to tangible assets. Food products are often outsourced to contract manufacturers and the price paid likely assumes most of the workforce would be eliminated—which suggests the brand might more reasonably be a far greater percent of the total price paid. Even with GAAP as the standard bearer, there's still no easy formula short of hiring a lazy accounting firm. We're working to build better ways to separate brand value from goodwill. Marketers deserve better ways to deal with CFO Linda.

REMEMBER WHAT YOU HAD FOR BREAKFAST, YESTERDAY?

CONCLUDING MEMORIES

IF YOU'VE BEEN SWIMMING IN THE WARM WATERS OF DESIGN, MARKETING, OR BRAND STRATEGY FOR MORE THAN A DECADE, YOU'VE INTUITIVELY KNOWN BRANDS HAVE VALUE. THROUGH SOME WICKEDLY INTERESTING MATHEMATICS, WE'VE PROVEN YOUR INTUITION IS RIGHT. MORE IMPORTANT, WE'VE PROVEN HOW RIGHT YOU ARE AND FOR WHOM BRANDS HAVE VALUE—SOCIETY, US AS INDIVIDUALS, AND BRAND OWNERS. WE USED THE FOOD CATEGORY OF PRODUCTS—IN BOTH GENERIC, BRANDED, AND NEW-ENTRANT FORMS—FOR A REASON.

FOOD REQUIRES A GREATER DEGREE OF TRUST, AS IT TOUCHES ALL FIVE SENSES AND EVENTUALLY GOES INSIDE OUR BODIES OR THE BODIES OF OUR LOVED ONES. SINCE COMPLETING THIS EXPERIMENT, WE HAVE STARTED EXPLORING LUXURY, TECHNOLOGY, AND A VARIETY OF OTHER CATEGORIES THAT YOU CAN CHECK OUT ONLINE. HERE ARE SOME PARTING MEMORIES:

1. The optimal marketing investment strategy and the current brand value would benefit from a new diffusion model that considers the micro-level activity of individuals and information specific to the brand and its place within its product category.

2. Every brand is uniquely situated, based on a large variety of factors that need to be carefully considered and modeled. There is no one-size-fits-all model for branding or brand valuation.

3. Brands acquired show up on a balance sheet, but those grown organically do not. Measuring organic growth of brand value would offer a large asset to leverage in an organization.

4. If your job is to build current and future revenues using the marketing discipline, knowing your contribution to brand value would be tremendously helpful in proving your value to an organization.

09

BRANDING + VALUE

THE SUN IS NOW SHINING BRIGHT ON YOUR BACK.
THE PATH IS A GENTLE GLIDE INTO THE FUTURE. IN THIS
CHAPTER, YOU'LL GLIMPSE INTO THE NOT-TOO-DISTANT
FUTURE OF A MARKETING CAREER AND THEN LOOK THROUGH
KANT'S EYES. WANDERING DOWN THIS PATH WILL REQUIRE
SOME CURIOSITY. WE HOPE YOU'VE LEARNED, TAKEN NOTES,
AND PERHAPS EVEN TALKED ABOUT WHAT THIS MEANS IN
YOUR ORGANIZATION. THE STRONGER THE BRAND, THE MORE
TRUST IT HAS IN THE OUTSIDE WORLD. THE MORE TRUST
IN SOCIAL RELATIONSHIPS, THE STRONGER THE FABRIC OF
TRUST IN A SOCIETY. BY THIS MEASURE, BUILDING A
STRONGER BRAND CAN BE MISSION-DRIVEN WORK, SO
KEEP PUTTING YOUR SHOULDER INTO THE EFFORT AND
CUSTOMERS WILL REWARD YOU WITH LOYALTY.

A COMMUTE INTO THE FUTURE

HOW THINGS CAN CHANGE

The trees pass by at just over 250 mph as you look down at a screen depicting the next engagement event for your new brand. You're on a conference call and cowriting the final plan for some new designed moments that a team of anthropologists, designers, and digital marketers have prototyped for your review. The voice of Linda the CFO enters the screen calmly asking you how your commute from Dunsmuir to San Francisco is going and whether you've had a chance to review her suggestions for your schedule and budget changes. The new brand moments have gained velocity in Door County, Wisconsin, and Pohang, South Korea, in the last twelve hours. You can zoom in and see data on individual customers and then zoom back out and see 153 metrics on your brand dashboard. Since you took the role of chief experience officer two years ago, the results of your team's efforts have proven to the board the future is bright for your next generation of food brand.

Peering up from the screen, you look out the window to see morning surfers and remember when big data was the center square on buzzword bingo. Your peers at business school were careening down a path of using marketing automation and intrusive retargeted online ads to bribe customers into buying. You zagged. Taking a chapter from the philosophy of the late, great Jobs, you sought to humanize marketing and use big data to improve the relationship between brands and people.

It's hard not to be proud of your collaborative and adaptive team of community engagers, purpose-driven brand handlers, design thinkers, and digital engineers. Each time you turn up the temperature of engagement in a new region, you see the data light up as if you're looking down on fireworks from the space station. Your team's ability to learn, create, and engage again is all over the latest social aggregators and international media channels.

Your personal digital assistant Sigmund—a great-grandson of Siri—quietly interrupts your daydream with a notice that the conference call with the new Shanghai office will start in five minutes. As you start to panic, Sigmund reads your heart rate and reassures you he will be the interpreter. He also notes the coffee table book you thought about ordering on the history of the first electric cars has just dropped at your front door, thanks to "one-thought ordering."

The ocean is on one side of you and old-growth pines on the other. As you brush your teeth and hair, your vehicle continues to glide toward your destination in downtown San Francisco, just over an hour of travel from Dunsmuir, 267 miles north. You listen to Linda as she presents her plan for how to socialize the brand in communities starting in Shanghai with the Chinese team. Sigmund comes back on to ask if you'd like to transfer Blockchain funds to finance the Chinese team's effort. Sigmund reconciles your schedule.

As you lean back and shut your eyes, you reflect back on your neighbor Amy, who launched a line of digital eyewear, who also focused her marketing efforts on individuals, the community, and the partners who handle the brand. Her quote still rings in your head: "Just as the movies aren't about special effects, marketing is not about the technology or the media buy; it is about the relationship we have with real people and the moments we've designed to make their lives brighter and easier." You watched her brand achieve velocity. You've been building on this philosophy.

Reality wanders back into your head as the vehicle slows and the call with your Chinese team closes with an earful of *xièxie*, "thank you" in Chinese. The 100-foot walk into the office is peaceful as your augmented reality eyewear filters out visual noise (billboards, transit signs, and other bombardment-style media) and your earbuds filter any audio sensory inputs you haven't approved. Yet a picture of a skirt from Uniqlo is allowed to get through and you make a note that it would certainly look nice for dinner with your husband. You can still use the best creative processing tool in the known universe, your brain. Most of the mundane tasks your brain once did have been handed over to Sigmund.

The day after your birthday, March 23, doesn't feel different, just another Monday in 2025.

CELEBRATE THE FUTURE WITH FIREWORKS

WHERE TO GO FROM HERE?

Brand owners have explored individual behavior in various ways for years now. What's new is the velocity, and even acceleration, that is expanding the visibility of individual and collective behavior beyond what has ever been seen before. Imagine seeing your next brand launch from the space station, and as each town sets off its own firework show, you see bursts of light explode and radiate in tight little clusters across the surface of the planet. Do a pinch zoom and go right into the fireworks as they go off just 100 feet below.

A brand owner such as CNN might see a similar map using data from those users of its smartphone app that have agreed to share their geo-data. As a news story at a specific location breaks, CNN can reach out and ask participants and citizen journalists to create video of the scene, and then help spread the word on social media, radiating light to their neighbors and friends across town. Suddenly CNN and the community are one, and news becomes deeper and richer.

Now think of other brand owners that are catching traces of your individual activities in databases. In our cashless society, new currency companies create a virtual map of your physical movements during the day. Their computers are running algorithms in real time looking for patterns that don't make sense, such as your being in two places at the same time. If something doesn't look right, you get a call to see if unusual patterns were your charges or a fraudster tapping your account.

If you need to return an item at a store, but don't have your receipt, at some retailers you can now swipe the credit card you used to make the purchase and scan the barcode of the item. The retailer's database keeps live records of each SKU that you bought for each purchase and will print a new receipt for you.

Direct-mail marketers have used micro-decision data to track household-level responses to solicitations for years. They use this to run tests of neighboring blocks to gauge the response rates from one version of a solicitation sent to one block versus a different version sent to the next. By using pairs of neighboring blocks, they control for a wide range of demographic variables. New methods for website design optimization use similar methods to randomly assign new visitors alternative designs of web pages. Once they appear to have a large enough sample to say which is more effective, they shift all new visitors to that design.

Some in-store smartphone apps reward customers with special discounts while they shop. The rights the customer grants when installing the app are that the retailer can track the geo-location of the customer within the store and see what other websites the customer accesses such as comparing prices with Amazon. A benefit to the brand owner is that it can watch micro-decisions being made in real time and integrate that with information from online visits and past in-store purchases. A benefit to the customer is that the retailer will give special discounts tailored specifically to the customer's interests.

It is more obvious how online retailers such as Amazon use its customers' past purchases and searches to provide relevant suggestions for future purchases. For most shoppers, this is a helpful feature and extends a brand's ability to improve their own decisions, reducing their purchase experience risk as well as saving money and time. Amazon's system of requesting and posting comments from purchasers of products are valuable to others. It also gives responders a social utility boost to know they are helping others.

These are just a few examples of the micro-decisions brand owners currently capture. These and other data could provide valuable elements of a systems simulation tailored to their own brand. An evolving system could calibrate to new behaviors and answer the big brand-management questions: What is the return on the current branding investment and how can it be improved? What is the optimal branding investment strategy in terms of how much, what mix, in what pattern over time? What is

the current value of the brand and what is the brand value potential?

You should be able to see the power of using a systems theory of brands for understanding why brands provide value to people, communities, brand handlers, and brand owners. You will also understand that the sources of value are multifaceted. Each brand's situation, history, and future opportunities are uniquely its own. There are no identical twins in the brand world.

Throughout this book, we have introduced you to three conceptual models: Jacob's Ladder, Time Dimensions, and Space Dimensions, which interact together in interdependent systems. We have created a complex computer program, Aurora, which illustrates people and brands interacting through time and space. We've shown settings designed to capture micro-decisions in the branded-food category emulating a hypothetical world of macro results corollary to the real-world results of our case study companies.

What does this mean for the future?

LOOK CLOSELY: THE BEAUTIFUL MAY BE SMALL

IMMANUEL KANT'S EYES

Start from the perspective of your brand's contact with human beings. People are people first, so seeing them as consumers narrows your perspective and fails to see the larger possibilities. All macro results are the sum of individual decisions, so look with fresh contact lenses at the moments individuals and their communities are experiencing with your brand. Consider intentionally designing moments to enhance your multisensory and emotional impact.

Use the systems theory of brand framework to get new perspectives on the many areas of specializations within and outside of your organization that contribute to building and managing brands and creating brand value. Hint: it's not just members of the marketing department. Use this framework to identify

THOUGHT EXPERIMENT

WHEN CUSTOMERS RECOGNIZE INDIVIDUALIZED SIGNALS ARE BEING DIRECTED AT THEM, WHERE IS THE LINE BETWEEN TRUST-BUILDING (HELPFUL) AND TRUST-DESTROYING (CREEPY)?

if there are any gaps in functions across the organization that are underserved or overlooked.

Make sure everyone in your organization understands the concepts of a brand and branding through customer experience. Make sure everyone in your organization understands the concepts of a brand and branding through customer experience. No, this was not a typo—we meant to repeat it. Since brands and other intangible assets often make up the lion's share of most companies' value, everyone should understand his or her role in managing this value. On the other hand, if intangible assets are not a large share of your company's value, why not? Even companies operating in "commodity" product categories like Cargill have discovered they can add substantial value with brands.

Prototype designed moments, perform small experiments, and watch for traces of responses in individual actions through the data you are capturing. Keep adapting and changing as the systems you operate in give you feedback.

Begin a process of financial literacy around brands for the executives and board within your organization. Undertake an effort to understand how the market values your brands and how that relates to the other assets of your company.

Consider whether you can use your data to calibrate key elements of customer behavior for a systems simulation model tailored to your brand and product category. Simulations can help you better understand how the systems interact, leading to better investments for your branding activities.

Ask what is the lifetime value of a person to your brand, not the lifetime value of a consumer—the difference is important. How do attrition rates vary by groups of people? What leads to that attrition? How much brand value could be added if customer interactions with high risks of attrition were redesigned? After seeing results, how much did it bring?

Visit *www.physicsofbrand.com* to extend what you have learned so far. Watch our videos and blog posts, and join a conversation with other readers to learn from them. Have an immersive moment in this new community.

THE ROBOTS HAVE A QUESTION

WHAT WILL YOU TRADE FOR PRIVACY?

Intelligent agents will be everywhere in the years ahead, embedded in clothing you wear, products you buy, and every computing device you touch. Data from these known, secret agents on the Internet will roll up into huge data farms where the "produce" from this farming will be sliced up and auctioned off to the hungriest brands. Historic brands still adapting to the social media revolution will need to catch this next evolution of the flywheel as it is picking up speed. The ability to make this next adaptation early enough will be reserved for those who learned from the last spin of the marketing innovation wheel.

The implications are monumental, with risks and rewards evenly matched for everyone involved. Except, of course, for zombie apocalypse survivalists living off the grid, with goats and a few friends. Zombie fear aside, there are reasons to be frightened as a person, and as a brand manager. Edward Snowden showed us what governments can do, and while our private data is being used to protect us, it could just as easily be used by tyrants to oppress us.

For brands and marketers, the prospect of all this data is mostly sunny with a slight chance of F5 tornados. There is an opportunity now to create communities of customers on your website, reach prospects online with pinpoint accuracy, have algorithms nurture and close sales, and then have robots pack and ship the orders. Amazon is serious about drone delivery systems. For lesser entities, there are huge opportunities for marketers to automate administrative functions, expand on the Internet, and build brand while forming deep bonds with people who purchase, repurchase, brag, and repurchase again. But here's where the F5 tornado comes in. If you don't protect your data and treat customers and customer data with the utmost respect, there could be hell to pay. Case in point, Ashley Madison, a social media network purportedly for married people seeking affairs. You could argue this is already an icky business, but evil begets

4.6 hours

Average amount of time people in the U.S. access their digital devices, daily.

87%

of millennials say smartphones never leave their reach.

1 in 5

people in the world are active on Facebook.

30 million

The number of entries Wikipedia has created, collaboratively.

2 billion

people globally have smartphones.

88%

of people say they have been influenced by online reviews.

100 minutes

The time Americans spend, per day online, for leisure.

15%

of Starbucks purchases are made with phones.

9%

of U.S. retail sales are online and growing.

4 hours

Amount of hours Americans spend watching TV daily.

THOUGHT EXPERIMENT

WHAT CAN YOUR BRAND OFFER CUSTOMERS ON THEIR SMARTPHONES AS THEY MOVE THROUGH TIME AND SPACE?

evil. Someone left the data backdoor wide open to hackers, who then stole and posted the names, credit card data, physical addresses, and sexual preferences of 37 million members. The breach also showed that the whole business model was a sham. The ratio of men to women checking messages was 13,585:1, and many of the women are likely what are called fembots—modern versions of a blowup doll.

MarTech is the new Marcomm, right up there with Content and Consumer as lifeless and boring terms for branding activities. Data can giveth and data can taketh away, but even with these risks, brand owners cannot afford to get too far behind the innovation cycle in marketing. That said, smart marketers are pursuing marketing automation and content creation with gusto. And the new skills for successful CMOs include abilities like SEM, UI, UX, HTML, CSS, agile development, content syndication, and big-data analytics. If this list sounds like a computer programmer wrote it, we agree. You can see why this is happening when you look at digital movement in numbers:

These stats are as of this writing. By the time this is printed, these numbers will likely change substantially. Future changes are projected to be nothing short of revolutionary. By 2019, more ad dollars will likely be spent online than on TV. By 2025, futurists predict that there will be $1,000 computers with as much processing power as a human brain, so we will likely have meaningful conversations with our digital assistants as we offload thinking tasks. And we will soon be pondering how much our brains are shrinking due to offloading our "thinking" activities.

Also, by 2025 futurists predict that there will be 1 trillion sensors spread across the world, providing instant knowledge of obscure current events. Set aside the high possibility we'll be picked up for work by driverless cars. These changes are projected to result in dramatic shifts in healthcare, education, and government, and, well, everything.

Back in 1970, futurist Alvin Toffler wrote a book called *Future Shock*. He predicted there would come a time when the pace of social and technological change combined with information overload would leave people suffering from shattering stress and disorientation. He could have been right in some respects, but the book is a bit gloomy. He did not predict that we'd have $1,000 assistants to help us think and manage our lives, or supercomputers in the cloud to make shopping an instant experience, or Headspace apps on cell phones that help us learn to be calm and mindful.

BRANDS IN TURMOIL, PEOPLE IN PERPETUAL DISTRUST

CHANGE BEGETS CHANGE

The humble printing press sparked the Reformation, played a role in the political revolutions of Europe and America, and led to the birth of early modern brands. Letterpress books and broadsides accelerated the scientific revolution and the development of what most call the modern age. Academics often say we now live in a postmodern age, where anything is possible and nothing is certain. Whatever you call this time and space, it is a period of rapid and dramatic change.

Most early royals would have likely traded in their cold and smoky castles for the comforts and conveniences in a typical middle-income suburban home. The kings and queens of old would be astonished by flushing toilets, light bulbs, automobiles, central air, refrigerators, and celebrity yoga on television. Brands and the innovations they fostered have delivered miracles and wonder, and by every account from respected futurists, we ain't seen nothing yet.

The digital world, combined with global trade and turbocharged computing power, is transforming the very land on which we walk. Many respected geologists call this the Anthropocene age, or "time of humans." Astronauts can see our changes to the land, sea, and sky from space with the naked eye. The earth is warming and species are disappearing, cities are booming, science and technology are zooming, and angst is looming. Religion is declining in most advanced economies while religion is becoming radicalized in the Middle East and Africa. Family structures are in flux and new technologies are replacing traditional ways of working. Some say this is the beginning of the end; others say this is the start of a new beginning. Time will tell.

Brands have a big role in this story, and that role could expand. Brands are islands of safety in times of uncertainty and resource constraint. As we've seen, brands save customers time, risk, and cost. Brands are also agents of community connection and global social affiliation. That's the good side of the coin. On the other side of this coin you have environmental destruction, social and economic disruption, and resource depletion. As they say, there is no free lunch.

Back in the 1960s, the counterculture had a saying: "You're either part of the problem or part of the solution." It's a bit confrontational and dualistic in our minds, but there is an element of truth in the sentiment. Brands and people live in time and space, and if people don't buy brands, sales and profits go down, memories fade, and then the best you can hope for is a footnote on a Wikipedia page.

Meanwhile, the U.S. Supreme Court has granted public corporations many of the same rights as flesh-and-blood citizens, and brands are corporate ambassadors. If brands are not good citizens, angry mobs could take away corporate rights. You don't want Naomi Klein and the editor of *Adbusters* magazine showing up at your headquarters with bullhorns and a horde of #Occupy insurgents rounded up on Twitter. The printing press zapped the royals, and the Internet is way more powerful than a tray of lead type and bucket of black ink. More to the point, in an age of frictionless Internet communication, word travels at the speed of light. These days, you can run, but you can't hide.

This could be the best of times for brands. The world has plenty of problems, and corporations and brands are good at solving problems. The great challenge is how to manage branding activities to create value for both customers and shareholders. Another challenge is how to create rationale for branding activities along with ways to measure the impact of branding activities on brand value. The previous pages will help you do that, and we'll offer some parting thoughts in this chapter. But first, a short address about the importance of humility, in our not always humble opinion.

WE'RE AT LEAST 95 PERCENT IGNORANT

BEGIN WITH CURIOSITY

Those involved in the hardest of sciences, the lonely physicists, admit we have no clue what 95 percent of the universe is made of, why anything exists at all, or what lies beyond the boundaries of time and space. Meanwhile, we can only perceive a sliver of the electromagnetic spectrum. We are smart about what we know, but stupid to think we can know it all.

Psychology is still a primitive field that is always undergoing revision because it depends on "social science," which will never match the precision of hard science (and even hard science is subject to dramatic revisions by people like Mr. Einstein). Neuroscience is a young field, and while we are making amazing discoveries about how the brain works, there is no universally accepted theory about how the brain as a whole works. This concept we have of a stable self has zero evidence for it and much evidence against it. We don't know what waking consciousness is or how it is formed. And although our brains are amazingly powerful, computers will be more powerful in a few short years. What computers cannot be is humble, curious, collaborative, and creative. Our very fallible humanity is our greatest gift—our greatest asset.

Just as the scientific mind continues to explore these boundaries of knowledge, we are seeking more conversations, evidence, studies, and fellow researchers interested in our structure on brands in space and time. Learning is our epic quest. Thank you for giving us a chance to learn

with you. We hope you have come up with some useful ideas along the way.

You've read this wearing a framed hat. You might not know it, but everyone comes to content with a point of view and a framed perspective. The challenge is reading while wearing a different hat entirely. If you consider yourself part of the creative services community, try reading it from beneath your customer's hat. If you're a student and read this from the perspective of a person and community member, take the entrepreneurial hat out of your closet and read it again. If you're a deal maker in mergers and acquisitions, consider what this means for the due diligence on your next deal, but read it again wearing your "individual who loves brands" hat—you know, the one with all the flowers on it. If you're an entrepreneur, you've likely read it with your brand in mind; try reading it again as a customer of your least-coveted brand.

ABOUT THE AUTHORS

AARON KELLER

Aaron Keller is a founding partner at Capsule. For more than 20 years he has led national and international brands through consumer research, marketing strategy, and brand development. The Capsule client lineup includes Target, The Honest Company, Patagonia, SmartWool, Jack Daniel's, Red Wing Shoes, Craftsman, and Leatherman. Aaron has an MBA from the Carlson School of Management at the University of Minnesota and taught integrated marketing at the University of St. Thomas as an adjunct professor. He's the author of three books and a popular speaker. When Aaron isn't in a seat on a plane, you're likely to find him on a bike heading across Iowa or the Rocky Mountains.

DAN WALLACE

Dan Wallace is the founder of Idea Food. He works with leaders to clarify long-term brand strategies and develop marketing plans. Notable success includes work with IBM, Korn Ferry, Apartment Search, Mindware, Pizza Luce, United Way, and the City of Minneapolis. Dan holds an Executive MBA based on systems thinking from the University of St. Thomas. The diverse books and blogs Dan studies guide his inquiry and insights into the brands he touches. Dan has won awards for branding, conceptual artwork, and innovation in leadership development. He is a frequent writer and speaker. When you don't find Dan deep in thought working to frame and answer questions for clients, you might find him lost in thought during a long nature hike.

RENÉE MARINO

Renée Marino is the founder of Cupitor Consulting, a firm specializing in the financial aspects of brands and intangible assets. Cupitor's services include appraisals, strategic consulting, and expert opinions in litigation involving claims such as trademark infringement and interference with customer relationships. Renée also writes and presents on these topics. She has an MBA in finance from the University of Chicago and sits on the Board of Governors of the American Society of Appraisers. She holds credentials as a Certified Public Accountant, Accredited in Business Valuation from the American Institute of CPAs, an Accredited Senior Appraiser with the American Society of Appraisers, and a Chartered Financial Analyst with the CFA Institute. Renée comes from a family of physicists and neuroscientists, but she zigged when the others zagged and ended up working in dynamic system modeling and advanced financial studies.

AURORA INSIGHTS

Aurora Insights is a collaboration of Capsule, Idea Food, and Cupitor. We work with clients to assess brands, develop brand strategies, and design moments to enhance brand value. To enquire about speaking or advisory services e-mail: questions@aurorainsights.com.

CAPSULE

Capsule's design provides a powerful tool for both understanding consumer culture and shaping it. Every encounter an individual has with a brand, whether a person, product, package, mobile app, retail environment, signage, logo, name, or website, can be a designed moment. Capsule helps you design a valuable experience for your audiences.